Praise for *Know Thyself*

"When Andrew arrived in Erbil, his presence in the classroom was palpable. Sitting amongst the children, he uplifted the entire environment with the spirit of only a true educator. Now, he has incarnated that spirit in the word and, with careful attention to man's design in the image of God (*imago Dei*), has defended the principles of classical Catholic education to parents, teachers, and truth-seekers alike."

—**Archbishop Bashar Matti Warda**, CSsR., Chaldean Archbishop
  of Erbil (Iraq)

"Scripture warns us that 'of making many books there is no end' (Eccles. 12:12), but Andrew Youngblood's *Know Thyself* is not just any book. He not only articulates a strong case for the classical renewal movement, but does so in a Christ-centered manner I've rarely seen even in Christian discussions of education, which are often distracted by, and settle for, merely political or cultural goals. Youngblood respects the giftedness and autonomy of students and prioritizes their needs, especially their spiritual needs. I recommend *Know Thyself* to anyone who wants to conduct classical education in a way that honors Christ."

—**Jeremy Tate**, President and Co-Founder, Classic Learning
  Test (CLT)

"Amidst a wide panoply of the wisdom of the ages, which may be reason enough to imbibe the teachings of this convincing tome, Youngblood really hits the mark with *Know Thyself* when he echoes the wisdom of the Holy See over the last 150 years. He calls us all, parents and educators, to a deeper understanding of and commitment to the true end of education: a personal encounter with Christ. Nothing less, in every subject, every day, should be our goal for our young people. I myself am deeply moved by his teacher's heart, summed up by his confession that 'I will not let my students define themselves by a college acceptance letter, a job, an illness, monetary success, or anything other than the love of their Father.' *Know Thyself* does a beautiful job at calling us all back to the Church's true vision for education, and showing how the wisdom of the ages makes this high calling not only possible but a fascinating adventure."

—**Michael Van Hecke**, President and Founder, Institute for Catholic Liberal Education

"*Know Thyself* is a pilgrimage of self-discovery through the world of education, and helps us think about our own education and consider our children's education. What is the purpose of education? Andrew Youngblood answers with his experience, expertise, and beautiful prose, explaining what we should know but have forgotten. Whether you are a parent, student, or teacher, this will clarify what Catholic classical education is and why it matters."

—**Nancy Carpentier Brown**, author of *The Woman Who Was Chesterton*

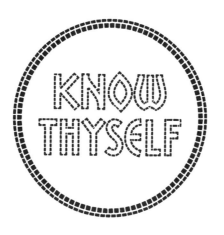

CLASSICAL CATHOLIC EDUCATION
AND
THE DISCOVERY OF SELF

ANDREW YOUNGBLOOD

FOREWORD BY DALE AHLQUIST

Published by Word on Fire, Elk Grove Village, IL 60007
© 2023 by Word on Fire Catholic Ministries
Printed in the United States of America
All rights reserved

Cover design by Nicolas Fredrickson, typesetting by Marlene Burrell,
and interior art direction by Nicolas Fredrickson

Scripture excerpts are from the New Revised Standard Version Bible:
Catholic Edition (copyright © 1989, 1993), used by permission of the
National Council of the Churches of Christ in the United States of America.
All rights reserved worldwide.

No part of this book may be used or reproduced in any manner whatsoever
without written permission, except in the case of brief quotations in critical
articles or reviews. For more information, contact Word on Fire Catholic
Ministries, PO Box 97330, Washington, DC 20090-7330
or email contact@wordonfire.org.

First printing, October 2023

ISBN: 978-1-68578-987-9

Library of Congress Control Number: 2022943562

To God the Father
for the Gift of his Love

Contents

Foreword

Dale Ahlquist

G.K. Chesterton says that the reason we study the *Odyssey* is that all of life is a journey. Hold on to that metaphor.

First, let's mention the fact that Homer's epic poem is not only still being studied after three thousand years; it is undergoing a surge of popularity in a growing number of new schools being opened across the country. In addition to studying Homer, students are reading more recent writers such as Sophocles and Euripides and Plato and Aristotle.

They are part of the revival of classical learning in intermediate and secondary education. While many parents, quite fed up with the state of public schools (and the private schools that do nothing but imitate them), are rushing to embrace this genuine alternative offered by a return to the classics, other parents are reluctant to send their children to these new "old" schools. They fear they will be too difficult and perhaps too elitist. But G.K. Chesterton offers this assurance: "The perfectly classical can be understood by anybody." And he lends further solidarity: "The tastes of the man in the street are classical."

But that might not be enough to put them at ease. For those parents who are still intimidated by the term 'classical education,' who are mystified if not afraid of such unfamiliar territory, Andrew Youngblood has written this book to help take the mystery out of it. He clearly and calmly explains what classical education is but also why it is vital.

However, at the same time, he paradoxically puts mystery into it. There are, after all, two kinds of mystery. There is the puzzle to be solved, as in a detective story; and there is eternal truth to be contemplated over and over, as in the mysteries of the Holy Rosary. Andrew fathoms the first and plunges deeper into the second.

Each student is a mystery. So, for that matter, is each parent. Chesterton says, "The self is more distant than any star." Studying the stars—as every student should do, just as the ancients did—only makes existence more wonderful but also more strange.

We first realize this strange thing called existence inside our own skin, our own mind, and our own soul. Thus the classical dictum "Know thyself." Who are we, and what are we doing here? If students are not looking for the answers to these questions in whatever subject they are assigned to study, then they are not being taught to think. The cautionary corollary to "Know thyself" is the profound reflection of Socrates on being sentenced to death for the crime of teaching philosophy: "The unexamined life is not worth living."

One of the main differences between the presently prevailing model of education and the classical one is that the present model keeps changing and is easily swayed by current fads and fashions, while the classical model is built on the real definition of education, which is to pass truth from one generation to the next. Our present schools are a hodgepodge of different subjects, some of which are deemed necessary and some optional, but none of which are connected to each other. But the classical model is based on an integrated curriculum. Everything has to come together. Chesterton says, "Thinking means connecting things." Modern education—and consequently, modern culture—has suffered by separating the arts from the sciences, the humanities from mathematics, language from its roots, philosophy from reality, and theology from—well, from the classroom altogether.

The three pillars of classical education are the transcendentals: truth, goodness, and beauty. If we pursue these three things, they will lead us to ultimate truth, ultimate good, and the beatific vision. As Andrew shows, the fullest and most complete classical education is one that is grounded in the Catholic Church, the house where the ultimates meet.

While Andrew Youngblood explains some of the reasons for the resurgence in classical education, he neglects to mention one: Andrew Youngblood. He is one of the reasons. He is the Director of Curriculum and Instruction for the Chesterton Schools Network, a growing collection of classical Catholic high schools in five different countries. Directors direct. He has helped deliver a carefully crafted, integrated classical curriculum to the many Chesterton Academies, especially in their nascent stages. He has not only had a front row seat; he has had a driver's seat.

That last metaphor was a good one. In fact, it gets back to the same metaphor that I asked you to hold on to. We study the *Odyssey* because all of life is a journey. Andrew describes learning as a journey. "To be on a journey," he says, "is the essential human condition." The goal of the classical, integrated curriculum is to arrive at a great family reunion at the end of that journey.

St. Charles de Foucauld's Prayer to God the Father

Father,
I abandon myself into your hands;
do with me what you will.
Whatever you may do, I thank you:
I am ready for all, I accept all.
Let only your will be done in me,
and in all your creatures.
I wish no more than this, O Lord.
Into your hands I commend my soul;
I offer it to you
with all the love of my heart,
for I love you, Lord,
and so need to give myself,
to surrender myself into your hands,
without reserve,
and with boundless confidence,
for you are my Father.
Amen.

Introduction

It seems a fitting metaphor that the path up the mountain was gradual, uneven, yet beautiful. The marble stones of the Sacred Way, elegant and refined, reinforced the sense of a pilgrimage. As he walked up this path, the man's gaze fell continually upon the peaceful valley below, covered by thousands of olive trees gently swaying in the wind and creating the illusion of a green ocean with soft waves. Somehow, this too must have reinforced the metaphor of his journey, for he was on a quest for answers, intellectual if not spiritual. As he turned his gaze away from the Valley of Phocis below, the majestic temple sanctuary came into view. He continued his pilgrimage up Mount Parnassus.

The details of his physical appearance are scant in ancient literature. It is possible that he was thin and lanky, resulting in an unhealthy appearance. But given that these details are recorded by a comic playwright who did not much care for him or his famous friend, it is entirely possible that this description bears the exaggeration of artistic license. Although well-known and a man of importance in Athenian society, his friendship with Socrates would become the trait for which history would remember him. In literature, he appears as a faithful companion to the controversial Athenian sage. And this journey, made with an impetuousness that was perhaps characteristic, was the most famous moment of Chaerephon's life.

The events that caused this pilgrimage are unknown. Perhaps his friend's tendency to be a polarizing figure in Athens was already becoming an issue that required some intervention. Perhaps he was overwhelmed, like so many others, by his friend's sagacity, or confused by the latter's constant insistence, contrary to his fame and reputation, that he was the most ignorant of all men. Whatever the reason, Chaerephon was determined to resolve the issue by consulting the Oracle of Delphi.

As he entered the sacred ground of the sanctuary, he continued his procession with the other pilgrims to the temple of Apollo. Believed by the Greeks to be the center of the world, the temple was famous for the cryptic, prophetic utterances that the elderly priestess, the Pythia, delivered in a trancelike state. It was her insight that Chaerephon sought in order to resolve the question that stirred him as so many others: "Was any man wiser than Socrates?"[1] Her eventual response that no one was wiser only accelerated the chain of events that led to the trial and death of Socrates, which would transform the life of the great philosopher's student, Plato. In turn, the life and teaching of Plato, and his equally famous student, Aristotle, would amplify the philosophical and scientific revolution that had been brewing in Greek society for over two hundred years and would officially birth Western civilization.

But all of this was in the unknown future. At the moment, under the warm sun, surrounded by the beautiful buildings of the sacred sanctuary, with the temple entrance in front of him, Chaerephon journeyed on his quest for confirmation of what he already knew to be true. Socrates and his relentless pursuit of truth

---

1. The reference to Chaerephon visiting the Oracle of Delphi is given in Plato's dialogue the *Apology*, which presents itself as a transcription of Socrates' defense during his trial. Xenophon also provides a version of Socrates' defense and mentions the visit. Chaerephon is described by the playwright Aristophanes in his work *The Clouds*. The phrase "Know thyself" was inscribed in the forecourt (*prónaos*) of the temple of Apollo in Delphi. Many associate the saying with Socrates, and both Xenophon and Plato mention that it was a topic of conversation that he broached on several occasions.

and wisdom had brought about this journey. But Chaerephon's pilgrimage for answers, if the first to be caused by Socrates, was by no means the last. Plato and, to a greater or lesser degree, nearly every student since would be impacted by the argumentative sage of Athens. And as he entered the shrine of Apollo, approaching the famous oracle, Chaerephon looked up and saw the famous yet enigmatic inscription carved in stone above the temple entrance: *know thyself.*

KNOW THYSELF

Education, both classical and non-classical, finds a stimulus and origin in the person of Socrates. He was a complex character, both inspirational and enigmatic, whose life and teachings marked a revolutionary new beginning in the Western intellectual tradition and in education. Since he did not write anything himself, we know of his life and teachings through the writings of his students, primarily Plato, and some of his detractors. When his friend Chaerephon returned from the Oracle of Delphi with confirmation that Socrates was indeed the wisest of all men, he responded not by boasting or celebrating but by trying to prove the oracle wrong. He set out to discover if anyone knew the secret of a meaningful life because such a person would surely be wiser than him. He began questioning everyone he could find, asking deeper and deeper questions about the important aspects of beauty, friendship, knowledge, etc., but no one could give him satisfactory answers. Instead, they pretended to know more than they actually did. Socrates began to understand that true wisdom came from embracing our ignorance. Only after accepting that we do not know can we begin the journey of education. Eventually, Socrates realized that the oracle had been right all along. He was wise, not because of what he knew, but because he was able to admit that he was ignorant. His methods of investigation, however, resulted in some noble and important men of Athens looking foolish. This caused him to be admired by some and despised by others.

His approach, today known as the Socratic Method, caused great polarization in Athens. He was accused of impiety against the gods and corrupting the minds of the youth, for which he was brought before the Athenian Senate. Plato's dialogue the *Apology* recounts Socrates' defense during the trial, where he stated that he had done nothing but attempt to prove the oracle wrong. The jury was not swayed by his argument, however, and convicted Socrates by a vote of 280 to 221. The law allowed a convicted citizen to propose an alternative punishment, but, instead of suggesting exile, Socrates suggested he be honored by the city for his services and be compensated for his work. The jury was not amused by his defiance and sentenced him to death by drinking a mixture of poison hemlock. Before his execution, his friends and disciples, including Plato, offered to bribe the guards and help him escape. He declined, stating he was not afraid of death. Socrates drank the lethal mixture without hesitation.

The life and work of Socrates did not happen in isolation. He was the product of a rich philosophical and scientific tradition that had been developing for almost two hundred years. But his brash and unapologetic methodology resulted in a rigorous search for the essence of things in a way that had not hitherto been utilized. His quest for wisdom inspired Plato and led to the creation of his school, the Academy, the prototype for Western education.[2] But even more than an inspiration for schools, Socrates provided a pedagogy and a purpose to education. He forces us to leave our comfortable lives and the safe places where we exist unchallenged and enter on a quest for self-improvement through knowledge. We are compelled to enter the dark space of accepting our ignorance and embracing the struggle to change. This can be a difficult journey, and one where we are constantly confronted with our own limitations, but Socrates has left us no choice. We must seek

2. Above the entrance to Plato's Academy was the inscription, "Let no one ignorant of Geometry enter here." The saying might be surprising to some, but it highlights the connection of Plato's school to the liberal arts and the integrated view of education.

to understand the world around us and, in so doing, discover the truth of who we are. We must learn to know ourselves.

THE RESURGENCE OF CLASSICAL CATHOLIC EDUCATION

For most of the next 2300 years, classical education, built on the principles of ancient Greece, was the accepted form of pedagogy and instruction. This changed dramatically in the late nineteenth and early twentieth centuries, when the principles of Socratic education were largely discarded. Within a generation, however, a revival of classical pedagogy began to take place. During a course on education given at Oxford in 1947, the English author Dorothy Sayers gave a lecture in which she applied the three traditional liberal arts related to language acquisition—grammar, logic, and rhetoric, collectively referred to as the 'trivium'—to stages of growth in students. Using this framework, Sayers set forth a pedagogy of education that transferred the structure of classical education to educational pedagogy and child development. No longer were the liberal arts only the *what* of education, but also the *how*. This lecture is seen as the starting point for the modern revival of classical education, a movement that continues to experience significant popularity and exponential growth in certain circles.[3]

When encountering classical education for the first time, parents invariably and understandably want to know the difference between it and the more prevalent pedagogy in public, parochial, and private schools. I had this same experience, but in reverse. Having experienced classical education in college and then working in classical school environments, I wanted to understand what non-classical education was and how it was different from the

---

3. The article in question is "The Lost Tools of Learning" by Dorothy Sayers. I agree with Shawn Barnett's article criticizing Sayers's approach, but the catalyst effect that the speech had is widely acknowledged. See his "Dorothy Sayers was Wrong: The Trivium and Child Development," Circe Institute, August 9, 2019, https://circeinstitute.org/blog/blog -dorothy-sayers-was-wrong-trivium-and-child-development/.

classical model when I was hired to run a classical program in a diocesan school that used common core educational standards for its classes. In order to appreciate the benefit of classical pedagogy, it is important to understand the difference.

One of my first observations, and one that I continually experience as a point of confusion when talking with parents, is that many people do not realize how much education has changed in the past twenty years. I had always experienced my exposure to classical education as somewhat consistent with my experience in parochial high school in the 1980s. This was one of the reasons that I was somewhat skeptical of all the chatter about the current state of education that surrounded the lightning-fast adoption of Common Core standards in 2010. Modern pedagogy, however, by its own admission, has a strong emphasis on job preparation and earning potential. This is markedly different from classical education in which the goal is to help students thrive not just at work but in the very art of living by cultivating a life of flourishing through personal excellence.

My basic experience of student formation as head of a classical primary school included aspects of mimetic instruction,[4] classroom discussions, repetition of core ideas for mastery, and integration of learning for enhanced student involvement and efficacy. An easy and straightforward example of these pedagogical principles included the use of songs in the elementary years for acquisition of grammatical knowledge in English or a foreign language (in the case of schools where I worked, Latin). They were fun and had a tremendous impact on recall. This allowed the students to have easy access to core information as their understanding of a particular subject increased. They could apply basic knowledge

4. Mimetic instruction is a form of pedagogy that engages the student through the journey of knowledge acquisition. It is a core practice in classical schools and comes from the Latin word meaning "to imitate." It is rooted in the understanding that learning is a journey that begins with an invitation and gradually grows into a mastery of new knowledge.

to material that was gradually increasing in difficulty, leading to greater and greater mastery. This did not seem very controversial or revolutionary. It actually seemed like common sense.

Other basic principles, such as the use of cumulative practice for ingrained knowledge of essential and basic information like math facts or consistent training through easy, age-appropriate writing exercises, seemed also undeniably beneficial. Assessing student engagement through kinetic learning, narration, or thoughtful conversation seemed equally obvious. Using constant monitoring of individual learning through some variation of seminar discussion with older students, which allowed the teacher continual feedback about where each and every student was with the internalization and mastery of new concepts, seemed to me to be the very essence of what it meant to be a teacher. It was confusing when I heard these techniques being actively discouraged and even labeled as harmful for students in non-classical settings. That is when I began to realize how classical pedagogy has a wealth of knowledge and experience to bring to the current discussion about education.

And this leads to a first observation about the discussion surrounding classical education. The discrepancy between classical education and non-classical education might arise from our unfamiliarity with the former but also with the basic principles of the latter. It is possible that people speaking about education today assume that there is little or no difference between classical education and current educational trends. If you went to Catholic school in the twentieth century, your experience might be more similar to the standards of classical education than most modern standards. In this case, it is not just classical education that you need to understand. It is how much education has changed in the early years of the twenty-first century.

MY JOURNEY OF EDUCATION

I graduated high school in 1989. Even though it was not classical, there were aspects of reading classical literature that were incorporated and expected within the curriculum. *The Federalist Papers* were part of my summer reading list for senior year. We read *Beowulf*, *Macbeth*, and *Crime and Punishment*. In religion class (I attended a Catholic high school), I was blessed to have excellent teachers who authentically and enthusiastically explained the Church's teaching. They succeeded in engaging the class—I was the exception—in seminar discussions. I remember the amount of effort, wasted on me, that my calculus teacher brought to his teaching of the material. Many of my teachers employed most, if not all, of the principles of classical pedagogy, called mimetic instruction, even if they were doing so unknowingly. After high school, I attended a large state university for one year. That was probably the closest I came to contemporary education: large auditorium lectures with small breakouts led by teaching assistants that were completely untrained at teaching, seemingly interesting classes that we could not sign up for, and core requirements that were arbitrary and disjointed.

The next year, I transferred to a small, Catholic college with a strong liberal arts curriculum and classical pedagogy. I never looked back. Everything about classical education worked better for me. It was engaging and interesting. It answered questions that were important that I had never thought to ask. And as I was exposed to Catholic culture on campus and intellectual rigor in the classroom, I felt myself being healed and made whole from all the lies of secular society that I had so readily bought into.

For the past twenty years, I have been involved with education, always classical, at all grades, from pre-K to college, and in various forms of leadership, including teaching, administration, training, consulting, and curriculum development. I have helped start more than thirty classical high schools, mostly in the United States but also internationally. One of my great joys was to bring classical education to a Catholic pre-K–12 school in Kurdistan, Iraq.[5] I have seen the impact of classical education on hundreds of high school students and witnessed the same healing that I experienced take place in them. Even more inspiring for me, as someone who works with schools that are both Catholic and classical, I have seen countless students be transformed by an encounter with Christ during these important and formative years. I see students encountering God's love, not just by the liturgical life or character formation of the school, but in the classroom itself, by the books that are used and the way they are taught. This is why I believe so passionately in classical Catholic education, and why I want to help you understand more deeply the riches that this education has for all students.

APOLOGIA (A DEFENSE)

I experience classical Catholic education every day in my high school classroom. It is inspiring, engaging, and diverse. It focuses on the whole child and unabashedly states that it is more focused on a student's success at life and their relationship with Christ than simply job training. It asks questions about the nature of love and friendship, law and civic duty, purpose and discernment. For those who are interested in learning about my program, I let them talk to the students. They are always my best ambassadors. And I am in a unique situation in that the students who participate in my classical program also take non-classical classes in our archdiocesan high school. So they are especially qualified to explain what they love about classical education and how they experience it in contrast

---

5. I have been fortunate to be the director of a classical Catholic program within a high school of the Philadelphia archdiocese for the past seven years. The program is part of a network of over fifty classical Catholic schools, and I serve as the Director of Curriculum and Instruction for this network. In March of 2022, I was blessed to lead a delegation that traveled to Iraq for its first ever papal visit and to help launch the Chesterton Academy of St. Thomas the Apostle at Mar Qardakh International School. For more information about this thriving Catholic school in Iraqi Kurdistan, visit marqardakh.com. Information about the Chaldean Catholic community in Erbil is available at www.stmiraq.org.

to non-classical classes. Some of them have provided personal testimony for this book.

Classical education also has its detractors.[6] They complain that it is impractical, outdated, or, worse, judgmental. These objections stem from a lack of understanding or misunderstanding of classical Catholic education. Others, like the criticisms that it is not in line with modern philosophical trends or that it is religious, are not only true but speak to the core of the mission of a classical Catholic school. Rather than answer these objections and criticisms, my goal is to lay out the beauty that I see in classical Catholic education as someone who has experienced it both as a student and as a teacher. I have witnessed the benefit of this environment on the intellectual, spiritual, and character development of hundreds of my students.

THE STRUCTURE OF THIS BOOK

This book is divided into two parts. Honoring the example of Socrates, the first part attempts to discover the essence of classical Catholic high school education by engaging in a discussion about the journey of education in general and examining the difference that faith makes in the educational process, before exploring some essential elements of classical Catholic education.

The second part will provide an overview of the integrated, narrative approach to education common in classical settings, using different periods of history as the starting point. The ancient world presents a time of longing for the redeemer of humanity, while the reality of God becoming man ushered in a new era and changed history forever, creating a Catholic society. A third period can be seen in the High Middle Ages, when faith and

---

6. A sample of objections to classical education can be found in a foreword written by Peter Kreeft to the book *Liberal Arts Tradition: A Philosophy of Christian Classical Education* by Kevin Clark and Ravi Scott Jain (Camp Hill, PA: Classical Academic Press, 2021), xv–xvii. The foreword, with a list of the objections, can be found at Christopher Perrin, "Dr. Peter Kreeft on the Benefits of Classical Education," Inside Classical Education, February 4, 2015, https://insideclassicaled.com /dr-peter-kreeft-on-the-benefits-of-classical-education/.

reason lived in a beautiful harmony in a Catholic culture known as Christendom until eventually, in the modern era, people abandoned an understanding of the human person informed by Christ's revelation to humanity. This rejection has led to an ever-increasing misunderstanding of who we are and what we are called to be. As these different periods are explored, aspects of classical Catholic education will be seen from across disciplines.

One final remark about the structure of this book: The fact that the arrangement of the seven chapters mirrors the seven liberal arts and that the first three deal with essential aspects (like the trivium) while the last four focus more concretely on the various subjects (like the quadrivium) is not accidental. But it also has no bearing on the understanding of the book. There are no hidden meanings or double entendres. It was just something I could not resist.

There are two main goals in authoring this work: to make the discussion about the benefits of classical Catholic education accessible for all parents and to give parents and educators a sense of what occurs in the classical classroom every day. Visitors are regularly shocked by what they see when they participate in our discussions. A professor from a local Catholic university sent two education majors to observe a Socratic seminar in our program. Afterward, they said they have never been part of such a dynamic discussion. This reaction happens frequently. When parents hear from their children about the classroom dynamic, I hear over and over again, "I wish I could join your class!" For those who are thinking about classical Catholic education for their family or institution, this book will provide you with context, background, and explanation of what this approach to education offers.

NO BOW TIES REQUIRED

I was having dinner with friends one evening. They were on the cusp of a big decision: where to send their oldest son to high school. They had narrowed it to three choices: an archdiocesan high school, a Catholic private high school, and a highly ranked public school. I was excited to hear about their discernment process and asked them how they felt the curricula of the three schools varied. They did not seem to understand my question and started talking about the quality of the sports fields and the cleanliness of the buildings. I persisted and tried to make my question more concrete: "What books do they read freshman year at the various schools?" I felt like I could gain a sense of how the curriculum was woven together by the answer to that question. Again they seemed not to understand and responded that they had finally made their selection based on the antique staircase in the main building. I don't think it ever occurred to them to look at what was being studied.

This situation is not altogether unique. As someone who is passionate about curriculum and who is repeatedly trying to explain what a classical Catholic education has to offer, I often encounter parents who are not that interested in the details of what is being studied in their child's classes. On the other hand, there are many families who are very intrigued by the specifics and are excited to discuss the curriculum. For those interested, they often quickly see the benefit of classical education.

There are many excellent responses to the question "What is classical Catholic education?" Unfortunately, they are sometimes complicated and often heavily academic. In videos, the men are often sitting in leather armchairs with thick bookcases behind them. Bowties are almost mandatory. A pipe is not unheard of. At conferences, a fedora or two might make an appearance. Women giving keynote lectures on the subject often appear elegant in ankle-length dresses. These are people whose work and ministry I greatly admire and respect. Although I eschew the bowtie, I am the king of the sweater vest, another staple of classical educational attire. To my great pride, my beard was once described as "academic." But an answer is needed for everyone, the men who wear bow ties and the squad of dads in their t-shirts and polos, the women in long skirts and the moms in leggings. The families in my program are down-to-earth, hardworking, and from a wide and very diverse set of backgrounds. They are very real and very busy. They care deeply about their children but have a million things going on. This book is for them and those like them.

Classical Catholic education is an amazing form of pedagogy and can be of great benefit. Through brief vignettes, personal anecdotes from students and teachers in classical Catholic programs, and examples from the classroom, my goal is to provide an explanation that is accessible, clear, detailed, and hopefully inspiring to all parents interested in helping their children find the approach to high school education that is right for their family. The book is designed so that you can read it in five-to-ten-minute increments if necessary. For all educators who read this book, perhaps the examples and pedagogical discussions can inspire you to incorporate elements of classical education in your classroom. It is a rich and rewarding approach to teaching, although at first it can seem somewhat daunting. If this book finds its way to students, then please know that, even though I addressed this book to adults, you are always in the forefront of my mind. Some students do not appreciate what an enormous opportunity high school can be, especially the learning experience in the classroom. But this is one of the most important times in your life. I hope and pray that your time in school is exhilarating, challenging, and formative. Don't be afraid to embark on the journey of education. You are worthy of all the best. You are sons and daughters of God the Most High. But it all starts with understanding who you are and who you are called to be. Know thyself. Your high school should teach you to see yourself through God's eyes. When you do, you will be amazed at what you see.

PART I

Understanding
Classical Catholic Education

What Is Classical Catholic Education?

The first part of this book comprises three chapters, dealing first with education in general, then Catholic education, and finally classical Catholic education. The first chapter discusses education as a journey of change. The learning process is fascinating and mysterious while simultaneously being natural and commonplace. It is communal by nature but must take place within the individual. No one can learn for another. As we will see in chapter 1, the story of *Brideshead Revisited* emphasizes how no one is able to journey for another. We hope to have the support and companionship of many on this path, but ultimately we are responsible for our own journey.

In the ancient world, Socrates highlighted the beauty and delicacy of learning by comparing the process of acquiring new knowledge to the process of delivering a baby. In this paradigm, the teacher is a midwife, guiding the student. This new life is always part of a student's potential. The teacher helps them make that potential a reality. But as beautiful and appealing as this imagery is, the reality of day-to-day instruction involves a host of variables that must all converge on and within the student for learning to take place. And this learning process that the student undergoes is a journey of change.

Literature is replete with examples and metaphors for the journey of life and education. Perhaps none is more beautiful than that of Homer's *Odyssey*, which illustrates the true nature and arduousness of a journey, the beauty of coming home, and the reunification that results. Plato's famous Allegory of the Cave is also a tale about the journey of new knowledge and one of the most influential parables in history. It is about a man who, through the enlightenment of education, discovers a new and more fundamental reality in the world. This basic message can also be found in many modern superhero and animated films, from *Iron Man* to *Moana*.

The second chapter explores how the Catholic faith changes the journey of education. How is the quest for personal growth through the transformation of knowledge acquisition impacted by the encounter with Jesus Christ? Quite a bit, actually. The fact that education is a search for, and an encounter with, truth takes on a much greater dimension when Truth itself takes on human flesh. This is why one of our most important tasks as Catholic educators is to create environments that facilitate this encounter. This is crucial at any time in life, and high school is no exception. If encountering Christ and building a strong relationship with him is our fundamental goal in life, then it must be an essential part of our educational journey as well. And since it is so essential, it is important to be direct and intentional with students about growing this connection.

Since the central reality of our life is our relationship with Jesus Christ, there are only two different paths we can choose: the one where we turn to Christ and allow ourselves to be loved by him, the other where we reject his grace and turn our backs on him. One relationship, two paths. This spirituality of the two ways can be found throughout Scripture and the writings of the early Church. Two paths, called the state of grace or sin in this life, result in heaven or hell in the next. There is no third path or destination. This relationship with Jesus transforms the journey of education into a pilgrimage, with one main difference: the goal is present to us as we travel. We need not wait till the end of our journey, of school or life, to achieve our goal. Christ is present to us in the here and now. In fact, we can only encounter God, who lives forever in the now, in the present moment of our life. The past and future melt away as we open ourselves to encounter our Lord in the present. This is why living in the current moment is vital. This reality must impact our decision about where we decide to go for high school. If encountering Christ is the goal, a good Catholic high school can provide the optimal environment for creating the space for this encounter.

I have read many articles and seen countless videos of people answering the question "What is classical Catholic education?" The definitions are not always clear and sometimes very academic. It is important that we are able to provide a concise and precise explanation of what a classical Catholic education entails. So the following definition is provided in the third chapter: *Classical Catholic education immerses students in the unity of truth, transforms them through a metaphysical worldview, and, through engaging discussion, encourages them to embrace a life of flourishing fulfilled in God's call to divine intimacy with Christ in his Church.*

This definition has several elements: (1) A classical Catholic education will present the various subjects in an integrated fashion. Truth is one, and learning, which focuses on truth, must be one integrated reality looked at from the various standpoints of math, literature, science, philosophy, the arts, history, and theology. A perfect model of this integrated aspect of education can be found in the first philosopher of the Western tradition, Thales of Miletus. (2) Since all truth is one and finds its origin in the work of the Creator, all reality shares certain essential characteristics of truth, beauty, and goodness. Known as the transcendentals, these essential aspects of all being help provide the student with a metaphysical worldview that is profoundly transformative. (3) The example of Socrates, who bequeathed to the world his famous pedagogical methodology, the Socratic seminar, is an essential part of a classical Catholic educational pedagogy—not because it is old and classic but because it is engaging, energizing, and healing for the students. Along with Plato and Aristotle, this great philosopher focused on what it means to excel in the art and craft of living. (4) Lastly, a classical Catholic education will have the Incarnation of Christ as the central reality that informs our worldview and teach students to think with the mind of the Church. If Socrates and Aristotle encourage a life of excellence, Jesus Christ transforms our understanding of the human person by promising that we are to be "participants of the divine nature" (2 Pet. 1:4). This promise serves as the starting point and ultimate goal of every journey, including the journey of education. Although these elements might be employed partially or arbitrarily in modern pedagogy, when taken together, these components provide the essential characteristics of a classical Catholic high school education.

Education

Brideshead Revisited is a strange story. The older I get, however, the more I appreciate the wisdom hidden within its pages. The book focuses on Captain Charles Ryder, an English soldier during the final days of World War II who finds himself at Brideshead Castle, the palatial family home of the Flytes, a rich, Catholic family he knew in the decades before the war. This unexpected return triggers him to remember his relationship with each of the six family members. Charles had been friends with some, distant with others, and intimate with still others. He had watched as the various family members worked through the struggles and obstacles of life as they journeyed on their own personal path of redemption. Some paths were straight and easy; some were messy and complicated. But Charles was there to witness as the members of the Flyte family worked out their own salvation "with fear and trembling" (Phil. 2:12). The ultimate moral of the story is that each family member had to discover their path in life on their own. They had support from each other, from the Church, and from various corners, but Charles was never able to do anything but journey with them. Even if he had wanted to, he could never have journeyed for them.

This is the lesson of *Brideshead Revisited*, and it is the lesson that I have come to accept at a deeper and deeper level as a parent and as a teacher, especially when it comes to my own children.

We can never acquire anything for anyone else. Sure, we can give, and more importantly, we can give of ourselves, to others. But accepting the love, guidance, or friendship that someone gives is not anything we can do for our children or our students. The same goes for learning and formation. At the end of the day, we can present or show information to our students, but that alone does not guarantee that the idea becomes a reality in their mind. There is an individuality that lies at the heart of education.

UNFORGETTABLE BEAUTY

Gregorio Allegri's musical adaptation of Psalm 51, commonly referred to as the *Miserere*, is one of the most beautiful pieces of music ever written. Beyond mere opinion, there seems to be some claim to the superior artistry of this composition based on its remarkable history. Written in 1638 for use during the liturgy of Holy Week, this masterpiece of lyric spirituality was reserved for use only in the pope's private chapel, known today as the Sistine Chapel. As a testimony to its beauty, legend has it that the pope decided in due course that Allegri's *Miserere* was not allowed to be copied or performed at any other time or place, under pain of excommunication.

In 1770, having established his reputation as a musical prodigy several years prior, a teenage Mozart was on a tour of Italy with his father. They attended the Holy Week Tenebrae services at the Vatican. Upon returning to his hotel room that afternoon, Mozart wrote a full copy of Allegri's baroque masterpiece. He might have returned to the Sistine Chapel a day or two later to verify that his transcription was accurate and to make small corrections. But the secrecy had been broken and the manuscript was published the next year.[1]

---

1. The story of the *Miserere* is more complicated than this historical legend. A more complete narrative is chronicled in *"Allegri's Miserere" in the Sistine Chapel* by Graham O'Reilly (Rochester, NY: Boydell & Brewer, 2020).

The story is intriguing and worthy of the beauty of the music. But it is also illustrative of what happens in education. For Allegri, the *Miserere* was a composition, an original work that he was able to communicate to others through performance. For Mozart, however, the hauntingly beautiful music was an experience. He heard the performance and was able to reproduce the communication that Allegri had originally used to ensure future performances. Something that happened *to* him became something that happened *within* him. Prior to that day, others might have been impacted by the beauty of the piece, but it produced a knowledge in Mozart that is evidenced by the transcription he produced. And to a certain extent, education attempts to do the same thing all day, every day: to transfer knowledge to someone new and create that reality within them.

NEW LIFE

At its most fundamental level, education involves knowledge transfer. For example, the student does not know division and they are now at the stage where they are ready to learn this unknown material. The instructor explains the concept and procedure, and then checks with the student for comprehension. After a certain degree of understanding is attained, the student will then attempt to apply the new knowledge to a practice question. Through repetition, the student's mastery grows. The new material can then be built upon and applied to various cases. In a sense, the knowledge from the teacher was transferred to the student and then grew to maturity within the pupil. And this simple example encapsulates the learning process of education.

But this illustration also highlights how complex the process of learning is. It is a journey of knowledge from one person to another, but then also a journey of transformation within the learner. It is beautiful and transformative, as with Mozart and Allegri's *Miserere*. So profound is this transfer of knowledge that Socrates likened the appearance of the new idea in another to that of a birth. In the dialogue *Theaetetus*, Socrates encourages a young man to attempt to understand the essence of knowledge. The pupil, Theaetetus, complains that it is hard and that he is unsure if he is up to the task. Socrates replies, "These are the pangs of labor, my dear Theaetetus; you have something within you which you are bringing to the birth."[2] Socrates eases his student's anxiety by reassuring him that he is able to guide him through this process, since Socrates sees himself as a midwife for birthing new ideas. "Well, my art of midwifery is in most respects like theirs; but differs, in that I attend men and not women; and look after their souls when they are in labor, and not after their bodies: and the triumph of my art is in thoroughly examining whether the thought which the mind of the young man brings forth is a false idol or a noble and true birth."[3]

Despite the male-centric phraseology, the imagery is fascinating. The acquisition of new knowledge is analogous to a birth, the idea being the new life that is born—not because it is new but because it is new to the student—and the teacher acts as midwife, guiding the process and keeping the student safe.

TO MOLD AND TO LEAD

There is a fortuitous vagueness in the etymology of the word 'education.' While it seems clear that it stems from the Latin word *educare*, which translates as "to train" or "to mold," the English word is also very similar to another Latin word, *educere*, "to lead out," which also seems appropriate in a discussion about the nature of education. Both aspects are present in the process of learning. Understanding how they both apply becomes easier when the various component pieces of the education process are distinguished.

2. Plato, *Theaetetus*, in *The Dialogues of Plato*, vol. 3, trans. Benjamin Jowett (New York: Charles Scribner, 1871), 348.
3. Plato, *Theaetetus*, 350.

Education begins and ends with the student. And I mean that literally, not metaphorically. The process of education starts with a student. The largest factor in determining educational success is student mindset.[4] But there are other behavioral factors that are relevant to the openness to the educational process. How receptive are they to learning? What baggage or obstacles do they bring to the process? Where are they on the knowledge acquisition continuum? It is up to the teacher to make this assessment of where each student is—not just annually or daily but moment to moment.

After assessing where the student is, the teacher comes into focus as an integral part of the education process. Unlike the word 'education,' the word 'teacher' is of Germanic origin. It means "to present" or "to show." Any teacher today will tell you that teaching, or education in general, is far, far more than simply presenting material. Beyond understanding the strengths, weaknesses, and challenges of each student, they must create a safe and healthy learning environment, guide the students through the knowledge acquisition process, and help them assimilate and integrate new material, all the while creating community, guiding the classroom dynamic, and managing logistics, grades, parent partnerships, etc. While it is not true that all of the onus of educational success falls on the teacher, it is also not untrue to say that they are the most important variable outside of the learner in the educational puzzle. That is why I like to talk about the "craft" of teaching. Teachers are artists. And great teachers make some of the most indelible and beautiful art ever made.

The classroom itself—its layout, design, amount of square footage, natural light—is also a component of the educational

---

4. The importance of student mindset is maintained in the article by Mona Mourshed, Marc Krawitz, and Emma Dorn, "How to Improve Student Educational Outcomes: New Insights from Data Analytics," McKinsey & Company, September 22, 2017, https://www.mckinsey.com/industries/education/our-insights/how-to-improve-student-educational-outcomes-new-insights-from-data-analytics.

paradigm, but far less important in terms of successful outcomes than people sometimes think. Technology is in the same category. It is potentially useful, but also potentially harmful, and has no bearing on outcomes separate from the way in which it is employed by the teacher. The administration has greater influence within the educational process than the classroom or technology. It is vital to developing the team, supporting the teachers, implementing the curriculum, and guarding the culture of the school.

It seems possible to complete the loop of education without mention of the parents. After all, in a sense they have delegated the molding and leading of their children to educational professionals. But common sense and the experience of nearly all teachers will confirm that this is false. Teachers might be called upon to teach long division, the structure of the cell, or factoring polynomials, but everything that happens in the classroom is an extension of the molding and the leading that happens at home. The formation that happens at school mirrors the formation that has been happening at home throughout the life of the student.

Eventually, all of these factors result in the process of the student being molded (*educare*) and led (*educere*). That is why education begins and ends with the student. A student arrives in a learning environment and, through the combination of all the factors listed above, is invited to go on a journey of knowledge acquisition. We are asking students to form new ideas in their minds that were not previously there or connect information that they knew but in a new way. We ask them, and guide them, to give birth to an idea or a feeling or an understanding that did not previously exist in them. That is the miracle of learning. And the journey that occurs between the start and finish of a lesson, a unit, a semester, or an academic year is what we call education.

THE JOURNEY IN EDUCATION

The learner is the center of the education process. Their journey from not-knowing to knowing is the essence of education. This process happens constantly throughout our lives, in little and big ways, and becomes formalized when we enter school. But a student, even when motivated, can still be passive in the learning process. It is something that happens to them. One way to allow students to be more in control of their education is to give them insight into the learning process. Thinking about thinking or learning about learning develops meta-awareness. One activity that I find effective for helping students improve outcomes on tests, especially standardized tests, is to teach them to analyze how a test is made and to show them how to make a similar test themselves. This way, instead of "taking" a test, they understand the structure, anticipate questions, and can assess what the test is trying to do and how well it is achieving its goal. It is always fun, after a standardized test, to discuss not only how they did but how well the test was made. Once the students can grade the test-maker, their own grade as a test-taker will often climb, sometimes considerably.

I have found that helping students develop this meta-awareness is one of the most successful educational tools. It allows students a sense of engagement and control in the learning process. Beyond increased success in the classroom, this ability to observe the structure inherent within something and to consciously choose our reaction can be applied to all aspects of high school life, including standardized test instruction, sports training, and friendships. In a world that often feels beyond their control, developing meta-awareness can help adolescents see structure and give them a sense of security. Examples of developing meta-awareness will be given throughout this book, but for now, we will limit ourselves to the topic at hand: the journey.

Besides *Brideshead Revisited*, literature is replete with the theme of journeys. Dante's *Divine Comedy* is a complete journey through the moral life and the afterlife; *Pilgrim's Progress* is an allegory of the Christian's journey to heaven. In the genre of fantasy, C.S. Lewis' *The Last Battle* describes our final journey and Tolkien's *The Lord of the Rings* trilogy describes the triumphant journey of good into the realm of evil. There are journeys, short and long, throughout Scripture, from the Israelites' journey to the Promised Land to Paul's missionary journeys to proclaim the Gospel.

There are also intellectual journeys—the centuries-long discussion of the philosophers, for example. There are historical journeys such as the Avignon Papacy that ended through the zeal and admonition of St. Catherine of Siena, the abolishment of the slave trade in England through the efforts of William Wilberforce, or the ongoing civil rights movement in the United States. Even a geometric proof can be seen as a kind of journey. To be on a journey is the essential human condition, and this is reflected throughout all aspects of a high school education. G.K. Chesterton, the witty and profound Christian apologist of the early twentieth century, has a famous summary of his own spiritual journey in his book *Orthodoxy*, where he describes the excitement of one who has gone on a long and perilous journey only to arrive back at home, realizing that home was where he sought to be all along. This is the story of the *Wizard of Oz* and many (if not most) animated Disney movies. But one of my favorite examples of the human journey, and the eventual arrival back at home, is in Homer's *Odyssey*.

THE JOURNEY HOME

The *Odyssey* is an epic poem from the eighth century BC. It gets its name from the titular character, Odysseus, as he travels home to his family following the Trojan War. Even though the title refers to a character, Odysseus' journey is so foundational in literature and Western civilization that the term 'odyssey' itself has come to mean a long journey. There are three aspects of the *Odyssey* that I think are poignant lessons for life's journey.

The first is the desire to be reunited with our family. Odysseus was reluctant to leave his home on the Greek island of Ithaca and fulfill his obligation to fight in the Trojan War, especially since his first child had just been born, and he tried hard to evade involvement through the use of his signature cunning. Obviously, he failed, and he ended up being the one to bring the ten-year-long military campaign against the citizens of Troy to an end (the famous Trojan horse was Odysseus' idea). After the war, his journey home, which should have been relatively quick, turned into . . . well, an odyssey, and one that lasted ten years. Throughout that time, however, Odysseus always yearned to return home and be reunited with his family.

Meanwhile, back in Ithaca, our hero's desire to return home was matched with the pure and virtuous desire of his wife, Penelope, and son, Telemachus, to see his homecoming. So strong was his son's desire to have his father back that he embarked on his own odyssey to retrieve him. Although she never leaves home, Penelope had perhaps the most challenging odyssey by maintaining the family estate from hordes of evil and greedy men. Using a degree of cunning that easily matches her husband's, along with a degree of virtue that far surpasses her husband's, Penelope is able to protect the family home, figuratively and literally, and safeguard a place for reunification to happen.

The intensity of Odysseus', Penelope's, and Telemachus' desire to be reunited stands in strong contrast to the family of Agamemnon, and this is the second lesson from the epic poem. While Odysseus' family longs to be together and displays an immense amount of loyalty and devotion, there is another Greek king who, along with his family, is highlighted in almost every chapter of the *Odyssey*, not for their desire to be reunited, but for their dysfunctional family dynamics. In a nutshell, Agamemnon's wife, Clytemnestra, is angry at her husband—understandably—for having sacrificed their daughter, Iphigenia, before the Trojan War (more on this later). When Agamemnon returns home victorious ten years later, Clytemnestra and her lover chop off his head. (I was not joking when I said they were dysfunctional.) This leaves their son, Orestes, confused as to how he should exercise proper filial piety: Should he give his mom a pass for killing his dad since his dad killed his sister, or should he kill his mom for killing his father? (At this point in the story—not to minimize anyone's personal struggles—I point out to my high school students that some teenagers have it rougher than others.) Orestes ends up deciding to kill his mom, for which he is tortured by the gods. In a surprising turn for Greek literature, there is a version of the story where Orestes is declared innocent by the gods and reunites with his sister, Iphigenia, who was protected by the goddess Artemis. That is as close to a happy ending as you are going to get in Greek tragedies.

So among all this dysfunction and carnage, what is the second lesson in the story of the *Odyssey*? Virtue, forgiveness, patience, and trust reunite families—earthly and heavenly—while vice, hatred, anger, and revenge destroy them. Not a bad lesson for a book that is 2800 years old, and definitely a great approach to thriving in high school.

But my favorite parts of the *Odyssey*, and the ones that I think have the most to teach us, are the reunifications that happen at the end of the poem. Odysseus has been gone for twenty years, so coming home takes a lot of reacquaintance and, in the case of Odysseus and Penelope, learning to fall in love all over again. There are several reunions for Odysseus, including with his son, his father, one of his farmers, his childhood nurse, and even his dog, Argos. Leaving aside the fact that this must have been one very old dog, it's endearing that the reunification between Odysseus and Argos is the most immediate and effortless.

The most complicated reacquaintance was also the most important: the reunion between husband and wife. The poem spends several chapters on the reunification of Odysseus and Penelope, and tenderly describes their caution, their fear of vulnerability, and their growth in trust with one another. The strength of their love is symbolized by the marital bed, which is carved from an unmovable tree growing in the palace. In fact, this is exactly how Penelope receives her final proof that the man in front of her is indeed her husband. With the signature cunning of their family, Penelope orders the bed to be removed, and when Odysseus forcefully objects that their bed is unmovable, she finally allows herself to believe that her husband has returned. In that moment, a family is reborn by the unconditional and patient love that they have for one another.

This example of the *Odyssey* illustrates the beauty and power of classic literature. Yes, it is old, but that in and of itself does not make it valuable or able to speak to me as a reader and as a person. It is the timeless truth that it illustrates that makes it valuable. Most of the classical canon speaks to the inherent human longing for truth, peace, forgiveness, understanding, and redemption. Its message is universal for all men and women, of all cultures, times, and places. Although often epic in scope, the classics are deeply personal and usually focus on the journey of one individual. And exposure to this beauty and truth in literature and learning can be transformative and healing for high school students.

Time and time again, I am struck by how nearly all high schoolers, by the age of fourteen, have developed a deep-rooted sense that they are fundamentally unworthy of unconditional love. It seems to be something in the DNA of young teenagers. Deep down, something (or someone) has convinced them that if God knew who they really were, they would be rejected. It is a shocking reality for me as a teacher and a sobering one as a parent. And I am not only speaking of children who have difficult home lives or challenging situations; this reality seems to hold true for most teenagers, even the ones that come from homes with loving, caring, and devoted parents. Reading and discussing books like the *Odyssey* with students gives them the ability to reflect on their own journey of life. The ultimate journey of every teenager, the one that motivates so much of the good, the bad, and the just plain dumb things that they do, is the journey to accept that they are known and loved for who they are, unconditionally and completely. This is the starting point of every journey of education. Even if they have never left, as Chesterton remarks, they still yearn to come home. Desperately.

Personal Reflection from a Classical Catholic
High School Teacher: Mr. Fadi

My hometown is beautiful. Latakia is a coastal city located on the Mediterranean Sea. I remember how powerful the green of the trees was and the crystal blue of the water. It was like paradise.

The day I left was the worst day of my life. War broke out when I was in 9th grade. I knew that when my studies were completed, I would have to enlist for my mandatory military service. There was war, so the choice was kill or be killed. I couldn't do it. My brother had left several years before to take a job as a chef in Iraq, so, after graduating from college with my engineering degree, I said goodbye to my parents and my sister and my beloved home in Syria. I drove to Damascus and took a ninety-minute flight to Erbil in Iraqi Kurdistan. I was devastated.

As I flew from my beloved homeland, I watched as the green and blue were replaced by the brown of the desert. I arrived in Erbil with no job. I was blessed to find work as a teacher in a local Catholic school. They were just starting a classical program in their high school, and I was hired to teach literature, philosophy, and history.

I had no experience as a teacher, and I was very nervous in the weeks prior to the start of school. But I was also excited. I loved the material that I was preparing, and I looked forward to learning along with the students. I used styrofoam to turn one end of my classroom into a Greek temple to help the students become part of the ancient Greek world that we would study for most of the year.

My first year is almost over and I can say now that I love teaching. I love the beauty of complex ideas, and I like finding simple ways to describe them so that the students can start to enter into these ideas and make them their own. It is fascinating to see them wrestle with new concepts from literature and philosophy and engage with one another as they share their thoughts and ideas. Together, they refine their understanding and apply it to other things we have studied or things they have heard.

This past year has been full of blessings and sufferings. Leaving my family and home was the hardest thing I have done. Learning a new profession has also been an odyssey with many challenges. But there have been many joys and blessings on this journey, with many new friends and new opportunities. And being with the students has been the greatest blessing of all. Learning and exploring with them. Encouraging them when they don't want to do any work! Reading and discussing with them the *Odyssey* and Plato's *Apology*. Guiding them through a discussion of the Allegory of the Cave. Their journey gives me life and hope as I continue on my own path to find my home in this world.

EDUCATION AS A CHANGE PROCESS

The journey to discover home is the journey of self-discovery. Know thyself. Acquiring new knowledge or developing a new skill requires the student to move into a new place, and this movement requires a journey of change and self-growth. And change is often scary. Few people have explained how complicated and difficult this journey is better than the Greek philosopher Plato in his famous Allegory of the Cave.

Known to history by a nickname, Plato's real name at his birth in 427 BC was Aristocles. He had a failed career as a wrestler—the nickname Plato means "broad" and possibly refers to his stature—and then as a poet. He was resigned to enter politics when he happened upon the itinerant philosopher Socrates. He quickly became a follower and spent the next nine years absorbing the teaching and method of his teacher. After the execution of his mentor, Plato traveled widely before returning to Athens and starting a school, the Academy. Unlike his mentor, Plato was a prolific writer.

In his most famous work, the *Republic*, Plato provides an example of the liberating power of philosophical learning in his Allegory of the Cave. He describes a world where all people are chained within a dark cavern. They face a wall where they see shadowy images projected, which are caused by fires behind them and objects moving in front of the flames. They have only known shadows their whole lives, never having experienced the full reality of the world outside the cave. One fateful day, a prisoner is set free and he exits his prison. The sunlight blinds him, and he is unable to see at all. Slowly, as he adjusts to his new surroundings, he beholds the real world for the first time. He is overwhelmed by the truth that had been hidden from him his whole life. Excitedly, he returns to the cave to inform others, but they reject him and his strange teaching.

This allegory is one of the most famous examples of the journey in education, and it emphasizes how dramatic the process of learning is. It is personal yet communal. In its essence, it is life-changing. And, in a sense, this journey of knowledge acquisition is the goal of education. But what is the ultimate goal with regards to the student? Once someone has learned long division, what then? Ultimately, the exposure to truth is meant to help students become their true selves. Yet we can only fully know who we are when we understand ourselves through the loving eyes of our Creator and Redeemer. Truth incarnate reveals to us the ultimate truth of who we are. And the truth of the classroom needs to point to this Truth. And that is why education is not complete if it is not informed by the revelation of Jesus Christ.

Catholic Education

We all remember it. The first day of high school. You went shopping for supplies. Maybe there was a summer orientation or you joined a fall sports team—both are great ways to meet people and get used to the new surroundings. But there is no way to avoid it altogether: there is a lot of anticipation and possibly anxiety before entering ninth grade. There is also anxiety for parents. And teachers. One reason is that there is a growing sense of independence for the students, and parents realize that their children need to start taking ownership of their journey, including their faith life. We can travel together, but our journey is always ultimately our responsibility. As seen in the last chapter, this is the lesson of the novel *Brideshead Revisited*.

This is why it is important to explain to students that high school matters not only academically and socially but also spiritually. Students, parents, and educators do well to understand that education is a journey. As we saw in chapter 1, we can glean important lessons about what a journey could and can be from Homer's *Odyssey*, which illustrates the importance of patience, forgiveness, and trust as we journey with others—important attitudes to have in high school. But ultimately, our journey is a pilgrimage, a journey with God and to God. As we face the new challenge of high school, it is important to turn and face Jesus Christ. And though we cannot directly give our children or our students a relationship with our Lord, we can create environments where they can more easily discover the love of Christ and build a strong and healthy relationship with him.

People speculate about which period in the development of a child is most important for cultivating this relationship. I do not pretend to know the answer to this question. If I had to give my opinion, based on the lives of the saints, I would say that they are all important. But the high school years, falling as they do during adolescence, are a critical developmental time for all young adults. That is why I believe high school is not fulfilling its ultimate purpose if it does not offer an environment where students can encounter the love of Jesus Christ.

JUST SAY "NO"

I was having a conversation with a religious sister who was superintendent of a large school system. I was emphasizing how we should be doing more in Catholic schools to tell students about the real possibility of encountering Christ. She agreed but had some concerns. "Isn't it dangerous to promise kids that they will have a personal encounter with Christ? What if it doesn't happen? Not everyone is going to have this experience in high school." Her concerns are valid and deserve an answer.

"No." That is the answer. It is not dangerous to tell high school students—or adults, or children—that they will one day have a personal encounter with Christ. We do not know when this experience will happen, but from Scripture and our faith, we know that it will happen one day—possibly in this life, definitely in the next. But it is also important to point out that having a personal encounter with Christ is not weird, exceptional, or abnormal. It is not something reserved for a privileged few, the saints and the mystics. Encountering the Lord in a personal and intimate way is the normal progression of any healthy relationship with Christ Jesus. Let me say that again: a personal and profound encounter with our Lord and experiencing his love is the normal progression of any healthy relationship with Jesus. And if this is the main goal of our lives as Catholics, how can this not have a significant impact on the way we approach education? How can an encounter with the transformative love of Christ not be the goal of high school?

FRESHMEN ORIENTATION

Students often give the same answers during freshmen orientation when I ask them what they are most excited about for high school. You can probably guess the responses: friends, sports, activities, classes, etc. One year, it struck me that this list was nearly identical to the answers that the seniors gave at graduation when we asked them what was most important about their time in high school. The one notable difference is that many of the seniors, year after year, would add one thing to the standard list: encountering Jesus Christ. It is one of the great joys of working in a Catholic high school where the administration prioritizes and works for this to be a part of every senior's list. The encounters our students have do not happen by accident. Many people worked very hard to help the students have this experience. But nonetheless, it's always beautiful to hear them say it and to realize that they have not just grown academically and personally but also "in the grace and knowledge of our Lord" (2 Pet. 3:18).

After realizing how the two lists differed, I decided that it would be beneficial to let the freshmen know that the most important thing that might happen to them in high school was not even on their list. So I developed a short talk about adding "encountering Jesus Christ" to their to-do list for the next four years. Even if it did not happen, it never hurts to be prepared. Since freshmen are generally overwhelmed by the beginning of high school, I felt that this message would resonate more coming from their fellow students than from me. So every year, after we discussed adding "encounter Jesus Christ" to their to-do list, I had several seniors give a brief witness of their journey during high school to discover the Lord.

On the day of orientation one year, we divided the freshmen, and each small group traveled to a different activity. My section, of course, was the "Is encountering Jesus Christ on your to-do list?" activity. When the first group arrived, we had our discussion, and I turned it over to the senior leaders to give their witness. What they said was powerful and overwhelming. They each described a specific moment over the past four years when they had encountered the love of Christ, a moment when their relationship with Jesus took on a whole new meaning, a moment that had changed their lives forever. To my surprise, two of the students described a situation where I had been present yet had not realized what was happening. I am not saying it was an accident that the encounters had happened. We had carefully and purposely created opportunities specifically for this grace-filled meeting. I just did not know that it had happened. It is hard to explain the feeling when you hear a student describe this important first encounter with Christ. It is beautiful and humbling. It is grace. And this is why I love teaching in a Catholic high school.

ONE WAY OR ANOTHER

The biblical book of Psalms is a collection of rich religious and liturgical poems that speak to the complexities of the human condition and of our relationship with God. The first Psalm touches on the core of the spiritual journey and speaks of two types of people: the blessed and the wicked. You could say "the good" and "the bad," although the Bible uses terms that are less about morality and more about a relationship (or lack of a relationship) with God.

The Psalm starts by describing the actions of one type of person. This individual avoids the company of wicked, sinful, and negative people. Instead, meditating on God's law fills their day. These two actions, avoiding sinful activities (and the people who promote them) while cultivating a prayer life focused on God's word, lead to being blessed. It is important to note that God's blessing is the result of our actions. It is not haphazard or destined by fate. The Psalm goes on to offer a beautiful image of these blessed individuals: "They are like trees planted by streams of water, which yield their fruit in its season, and their leaves do not wither. In all that they do, they prosper" (Ps. 1:3). By avoiding sin and growing our life of prayer, we develop solid roots, and we soak up all the life-giving properties from several "streams" of water. We produce fruit that can be life-giving for others, and we build a resistance to decay. It is a very simple and powerful image.

"The wicked are not so," continues the Psalm (Ps. 1:4). In contrast to the blessed, who are solidly grounded and bearing fruit, the wicked are compared to chaff, the parts of a cereal plant that are inedible. Chaff is a waste product that is left on the ground, and it becomes dry and brittle. It is not rooted and is easily blown by the wind. The Psalm does not tell us specifically what the wicked have done, although it seems a fair bet that they are not meditating on the law of the Lord "day and night" (Ps. 1:2). Rather, the Psalm focuses on the consequences of being wicked: they will not be able to survive judgment or be counted among the righteous. Their path "will perish" and is unknown to God (see Ps. 1:5–6).

The Psalm is beautiful in its simplicity—but also jarring. It seems very black and white. What about all those situations in daily life, so often complex, that point to the gray zone? Are there really only two paths, two ways? Scripture and Church teaching are very consistent: Yes. There are only two paths. If you are not on one, you are on the other. There is no middle ground. Given this reality and the importance of our relationship with Christ as the center of our lives, education that is not informed by the faith and directed to the same goal as our life of grace fails in every way to form a student in the truth.

THE *DIDACHE*

One of the earliest Christian texts that did not make it into the Bible is called the *Didache*, which is the Greek word for "teaching." It was believed to have been the teaching of the Twelve Apostles, like the first catechism of the Church. This explains its longer title, *The Lord's Teaching Through the Twelve Apostles to the Nations*. Given the prevalence of the spirituality of the two ways in Scripture, the beginning of the *Didache* is not a surprise. The first chapter is entitled "The Two Ways and the First Commandment":

> There are two ways, one of life and one of death; and great is the difference between the two ways.
>
> This is the way of life: "First you shall love God who made you, secondly, your neighbor as yourself; and whatever you would not like done to you, do not do to another."[1]

After several chapters explaining how to live the way of life, the *Didache* lists several sins that lead to the way of death. The short treatise then goes on to describe the importance of prayer, the sacraments of Baptism and the Eucharist, and guidelines for the structure of the early Church as well as for celebrating Mass on the Lord's Day after confessing one's transgressions. These directives were intended to help the early Christian Church live a life of intimacy and holiness, and many of the guidelines that they give are the same for us today.

The reality of an intimate relationship with Jesus, and the importance of encountering the love of God in a deep and transformative way, is a central reality of our faith in a personal, loving God. Too often the importance of this reality gets overlooked while we focus on the basic question of turning to God or away from him. But this first moment of conversion is just the beginning of an exciting and beautiful pilgrimage, one that should bring us closer and closer each day to the transforming love of Christ.

God exists, and the Incarnation is the most important moment of the human story. Accepting this truth is the first step; growing

---

1. *Didache*, or *Teaching of the Twelve Apostles*, in *The Fathers of the Church*, vol. 1, *The Apostolic Fathers*, trans. Francis X. Glimm, Joseph M.-F. Marique, and Gerald G. Walsh (Washington, DC: The Catholic University of America Press, 2008), 171.

in this relationship is the second. But we cannot content ourselves with just a friendship with Jesus Christ, no matter how amazing that sounds. We are created for more, for a love so intense and so intimate that the image that God constantly uses throughout Scripture to describe it is that of the intimacy of marriage. This is the constant message of the Bible: God wants to marry you and have a relationship with you that is so intense it surpasses everything we might have imagined. As St. Paul wrote to the Corinthians, "What no eye has seen, nor ear heard, nor the human heart conceived, what God has prepared for those who love him" (1 Cor. 2:9).

THE MOMENT OF TRUTH

If we decide one day to go on a hike, we probably have a specific destination in mind. Perhaps it is a trail or a special overlook with a spectacular view of the hills and valleys below. As we journey on the path, we are accompanied by friends and soak in the sunshine along the way. Perhaps we take time to enjoy the beauty around us as we head for the mountain summit. This is an earthly journey. A pilgrimage is similar, but also different. And the essential difference is that, although we are traveling to a destination, the destination already exists in the present moment. Our path is our destination.

Many of us suffer from what has become known as destination anxiety.[2] This is the idea that if I only achieve some goal, or win some game, or lose this much weight, or have those friends, then I will be happy. In this scenario, happiness, along with our destination, is always something in the future, something that does not exist right now. The problem with destination anxiety is that our goals have a way of shifting on us. When we finally reach the goal we thought would make us happy six months ago, we realize

2. To learn more about the history of the term 'destination anxiety,' or its more severe form as 'destination addiction,' see Mark D. Griffiths, "The Search for Happiness," *Psychology Today*, July 20, 2016, https://www.psychologytoday.com/us/blog/in-excess/201607/the-search-happiness.

there is now a new goal that needs to be obtained before we can truly be happy. It sounds exhausting, and it is. But we all have the temptation to think this way. Even the notion that "I will finally be happy in heaven" has a hint of destination anxiety. But at its core, this constant desire for a future happiness is a lie that misses the point of the present now.

In Sunday School growing up, I learned over and over that God lives in an eternal now. Later on, my theological studies confirmed this truth and explored this mystery in depth. But really, the mystery of eternity is not that God lives in an eternal now, but that we, just like God, only ever live in the now as well. Think about it. All I ever have is right now. The past, whatever it was, only impacts me at this moment. And the same goes for the future: all the excitement, anxiety, worry, planning, and anticipation I have about the future only exists right now. Those feelings say nothing about what is actually going to happen. Right now is all that counts. In this way, our lives are similar to God: we only live in the present. Granted, for God, the present includes the past and the future, but, to a lesser extent, our present also includes the past and the future. That is why our journey is sacred. Yes we are moving to a destination, but we live that destination right now. The grace that will overwhelm and surround us in heaven is present to us at this very moment. My path is not to Christ, but into Christ, and he is already present in me. This is the real journey. This is the pilgrimage of life.

The deciding moment therefore is not when we arrive some-where, but when we decide to start a journey with Christ. Once we commit to live our lives facing God and not with our backs to God, then the real adventure begins. That is why we spend so much time with our high school students on this moment of turning to face Christ. It is a moment of conversion, a moment of encounter. There is a word in Greek, *kairos*, that means the important moment, the decisive time, the critical juncture. In order to help students commit to discovering Christ in their lives, we focus on this *kairos* moment, creating a space and a time for them to have this opportunity to turn to Christ.

———※———

Reflection from a High School Campus Minister:
Fr. John Masson

During high school, I was one of the good kids, helping out with service clubs and ministry. I felt that I knew God, and I talked to him (or at him) sometimes. Several people challenged me to think about the priesthood, but this made me really angry. I had a girlfriend! I wanted a large family! So I started to avoid prayer and to avoid God. We had different ideas about my life, and I resented him for it.

I went on a school retreat my senior year. I had an overwhelming experience of love from my family and friends, and that opened me up to the love of God. I started to talk to him in a way that I had never done before, and I encountered him in a whole new way. When I opened myself to him and began to talk with him, I immediately felt his call to the priesthood again. It was annoying, but I didn't turn away. Instead, I opened up more. "God, I don't know you. How can I serve you?" I confessed. In my head and in my heart, God responded, "So get to know me."

I have been ordained now for nearly a decade. Most of that time I have been a campus minister in a high school. I'm not going to lie, it can be pretty frustrating. We work hard to create opportunities for kids to turn to God or to grow closer to him. It's hard to watch them make bad choices instead, or to slide back into bad behaviors. But they are on a journey, and all we can do is encourage them to say yes to a relationship with Jesus—and get to know him.

It's not surprising that the thing I think is most important is the senior retreats. We do a particular form of retreat called Kairos, and it's amazing to see the transformation in the kids.

Once they are able to trust that they are loved, they start to open up and become vulnerable in their small group. They receive so much love and support in their small group that they open themselves up, either just a little or a lot, to the love of Christ. That is when we start to see the miracles happen. These teenagers, who put on masks and build up walls every day and everywhere to protect themselves, learn to be vulnerable in a way they rarely have allowed themselves to be before. They start talking to God, praying at Adoration, and often, having the best confession of their lives so far. I see it in their faces as they unburden themselves in confession. You can see it in their shoulders as they let go and let God. Kairos was a powerful experience for me, and now I get to witness that same love transforming the lives of our students.

One of the things that is so impactful about the retreat experience is that you open a space and time for students to think and feel and connect. So much of our lives—high school students' especially—are spent on the phone or on the computer. There is rarely time to just be. Every moment of every day is full. And if we have a free second, we go to our phone or other distractions. The retreat allows the students to have a sacred space and a consecrated time. At first, it's a little frightening for them, but most end up loving it. The spiritual life is a journey full of twists and turns, starts and stops. But it is my joy and my calling to walk with our students and point them in the right direction.

I love my job. It is what I am called to do. Like I said, it can be frustrating, and it is often exhausting. But there is nothing better than watching others fall in love with Christ. Jesus is not just our destination; he is the way itself. So what's stopping you? What are you waiting for? Get to know him!

WHERE WE GO MATTERS

When I was head of school at a classical primary school, I remember board members saying that, if we did our job correctly, students should be sufficiently well formed in their faith so that it would not matter where they went to high school. I heard people say the same thing when I worked at a high school: if we formed the students correctly, they should be sufficiently grounded in their faith to go to any college, religious or secular. I think the whole mentality that emphasizes being "sufficiently formed" is wrong and sees our spiritual journey as two-dimensional as opposed to the very active, always-evolving relationship that the life of faith really is. The truth is that no one is ever "sufficiently formed" and the journey of faith is seldom easy.

The environment and the people that surround us are always important, and we should always strive to ensure that our circumstances are supportive of our faith. This is especially true when students are growing into adulthood. By virtue of the fact that we are not adults and in school, we are still in a phase of formation and not ready to exercise our faith independently. Actually, as members of the Church, the Body of Christ, and the communion of saints, we never live our spiritual lives independently, but as adults there is a greater degree of maturity that is not present when we are growing toward adulthood. That is why I think, as much as it is logistically and financially possible, we should always consider Catholic education as the first option for our school choice.

But that is somewhat of an oversimplification. Not all Catholic schools—be they grade schools, high schools, or universities—are successful at implementing a fully integrated, healthy, and robust Catholic environment. And in some instances, a wishy-washy Catholic school might be more detrimental to our academic progress and growth in the life of faith than a secular school. The exponential growth of classical Catholic schools taking place at the present moment aims at providing environments that are completely immersed in and informed by the faith, not only in the communal life, but also in the academic journey in every classroom. As we think about what schools to attend, however, it is important to remember that our relationship with Christ is always personal and individual. You always need to make an effort and to show up and choose the relationship for yourself. No environment will do the work for us. There are no guarantees, autopilot, or easy answers when it comes to living a strong and healthy relationship with Christ in the Church.

THE CASE FOR TRUTH

Students often go day-to-day with their classes, not spending much time reflecting on how the material in a class is connected and even less time on how the material in their various classes is related to form one search for truth. I have even known some teachers (in Catholic schools!) who tell their students that there are different truths for science and for religion and that these truths disagree. It is shocking how wrong and uninformed this relatively widespread notion is and how dangerous it is for the spiritual growth of students. God created one reality that has one consistent, multifaceted, rich, and beautiful truth. When people talk about multiple truths, what they are really doing is saying that reality has a truth that is separate from God, usually because they do not have much belief in God or understand the world in light of its Creator.

As someone who writes curriculum, I get to build a story that takes place throughout the four years of high school, spans all the classes in a given year, and goes more and more in depth from year to year. These horizontal and vertical arcs are part of the integrated experience that is essential in classical pedagogy. And when all of the classes are working together to bring the students into an encounter with truth, the Catholic identity of a school coalesces and becomes a positive environment for encountering Christ, who is the ultimate truth of the world and of our lives. This in turn changes students' attitudes toward their educational experience.

They strive for excellence in their personal, academic, and spiritual lives, not because of the college that it will allow them to attend or the job that they will someday have. They dive into the journey of education because they are called to excellence. God's love for us rules out any possibility of settling for mediocrity. In fact, if there is anything that is antithetical to our faith, it is mediocrity. And that truth informs our educational environment.

Classical Catholic Education

The difference is easy to see. We all know what the traditional classroom looks like. Upon entering, we are greeted by the familiar rows of desks that many of us remember all too well. Some teachers still use the age-old system of alphabetical order. Because my last name starts with a *Y*, I was always in the far-back corner during my classes in high school. Contemporary non-classical classrooms sometimes adopt cluster seating, popular in elementary settings but also appearing in high schools. Here tables or desks are grouped together to encourage group work.

The classical classroom looks very different. Rather than rows of desks, there are tables connected in a U-shape or rectangle with all the students facing each other to facilitate seminar discussion. This difference in classroom setup reflects the difference in pedagogy. In a non-classical setting, rows of desks facing the teacher and the board emphasize lecture-based learning. Textbooks are almost always utilized. Student interaction is not the essential aspect of non-classical pedagogy. Rather, the knowledge acquisition process is focused on the teacher teaching. In the classical classroom, the arrangement of the tables indicates the importance of the student discussion and involvement in the learning process.

This visual difference highlights the underlying distinctions between classical and non-classical learning. But the pedagogical difference can also be seen in more subtle ways. The purpose and use of assessments also varies significantly between non-classical and classical learning. Knowledge acquisition is a growth process that starts with the understanding of concepts, growing to an internalization of the material and some level of mastery, commitment to memory, and connection to other learned material. Generally speaking, this internalization and mastery are the result of repetition. The greater the frequency, intensity, and length of the repetition process, the greater the retention of the material and ability to apply it to new and different scenarios with ease and confidence. Classical education excels at both the initial comprehension of new material as well as the long-term internalization and mastery of concepts because the essential characteristics of a classical pedagogy do both naturally and efficiently.

THE ELEVATOR PITCH

People who have been exposed to classical Catholic education know how beautiful and successful it is as an approach to forming students. Although anecdotal, during my twenty years of teaching, and especially during my many years working in a high school, I have seen students achieve remarkable results, both academically and personally. But this observation needs some qualification. Some students are naturally gifted when it comes to the realm of school learning. These students have done well throughout their academic career, they do well on standardized tests, and, generally speaking, they have natural executive functioning skills. In my estimation, they account for about 25 percent of students. When I say that classical education produces remarkable results, I am not speaking solely about this group.

Most of education is geared toward the 50 to 60 percent of students in the middle range. These students vary in their strengths and areas of challenge. Classical education works very well with this group since it is naturally differentiated and can help build foundational skills that are lacking for accelerated future growth. There are also a group of students who have academic challenges and/or are in need of remediation. It is with this group that I see the most exciting transformations. So when I say that I have seen remarkable results, it is with all three groups simultaneously. This is one of the strongest aspects of classical learning. It is naturally differentiated, meaning it can build different skills in different students working at the same time.

On average, I have seen students experience a year and a half of academic progress in an academic calendar year. As a teacher, there is nothing more rewarding than seeing a student in need of remediation experience three to four years of academic growth in one year. I have seen it many times. In my opinion, it speaks to the power of classical education.

But, as convinced as those with experience of this amazing pedagogy are, it is difficult to answer the question "What is classical Catholic education?" succinctly. Any definition will have to speak to the unity of truth in the various and varied fields of study and how all learning is one impulse for knowledge that leads to one encounter with truth. Central to a definition will be the understanding that reality is permeated by truth, goodness, and beauty. The definition will need to highlight the role of human experience in history as well as the importance of the interpersonal experience of a seminar approach to learning. God's love as the ultimate goal of formation and the role of his Church as the guide on that path are also essential elements that would need to be mentioned. But as difficult as the task may be, it is important that we do exactly that: provide a straightforward and engaging answer to a complex question. So here it goes: *Classical Catholic education immerses students in the unity of truth, transforms them through a metaphysical worldview, and, through engaging discussion, encourages them to embrace a life of flourishing fulfilled in God's call to divine intimacy with Christ in his Church.*

The rest of this chapter will explore each of these elements in detail.

AN INTEGRATED APPROACH:
THALES OF MILETUS

One of the consistent hallmarks of a classical Catholic education is that it integrates the various areas of study into one interconnected search for truth. Classical schools will often focus on one historical time period and explore math, science, literature, art, theology, writing, and music from this vantage point. By thus integrating the subject material, classical schools create a learning environment that is harmonious and connected for the students. This provides not only greater efficiency in the pedagogical model but also a narrative to education that is missing from modern models of learning. This approach is not novel. In fact, it stems from the birth of education in the Western world.

The people and literature of the ancient world have been a guide through this discussion of classical Catholic education. There are some complaints about the study of the ancient world, however. The people that are most often mentioned are old, dead, white men, some criticize. This is only partially true. I mean, the part about them being dead is definitely true. There is no question about that. Some of them lived to be old. And most—but not all—of the people mentioned are men. There are many amazing women in the period that we call antiquity. Tamar, Deborah, and Ruth in the Old Testament are awesome heroines. We already mentioned Penelope as a literary hero in the *Odyssey*, and there are many others like Antigone and Iphigenia. And there are many female rulers who are also fascinating. So it is not just men that get talked about in the ancient world, although admittedly, the figures that are studied are disproportionately male by an enormously wide margin. But the idea that everyone was white is curious to me. Many of the people of the ancient world were from northern Africa or the Middle East. The Pharaohs of Egypt, the people and leaders of the Babylonian and Persian empires, famous authors and mathematicians like St. Augustine and Pythagoras, and biblical figures like Moses, David, and Jesus were not Caucasian. And the same might be the case for the father of all education—the man to whom is given the title of the first philosopher and scientist. A man known for his advances in math and his cunning in business. A man who, on top of everything else, was religious, yet revolutionary in the way he saw religion. And this man was Thales of Miletus.[1]

In the ancient world, the country of Greece was not contained to just the country that we know today. Greece was a collection of colonies that also included areas in modern-day Turkey. This was not only because of the conquest of Alexander the Great and the way he spread Greek culture throughout the ancient world. Even hundreds of years before Alexander, many areas outside of present-day Greece were considered part of the Greek world. This included the town of Miletus.

Miletus was located on what today is the coast of Turkey. For hundreds of years, it existed as a seafaring town and flourished because of its protected harbor. In the ancient world, it was considered one of the most important cities. Not too far from the city of Miletus was the Maeander River, a long and winding river in southwestern Turkey that feeds into the Aegean Sea (which is part of the Mediterranean). The Maeander River is so winding that our English verb "to meander" is derived from the name of this waterway. The problem for the inhabitants of that area was that the Maeander River was depositing silt into the sea, slowly making the inlet where Miletus was located disappear. This was not a fast process, but during the life of Thales, the Greeks of Miletus were documenting the encroaching land formation from the river. Since their livelihood was primarily based on their harbor, this

---

1. For more information on Thales, see Dr. Ron Gaudio's article "25. Thales Determines that Water is the Source of Everything," The Socratic Journey of Faith and Reason, December 15, 2020, https://socratesjourney.org/thales-of-miletus-water/. For a fascinating discussion on the importance of classical education for the African-American community, see the *Wall Street Journal* op-ed by Angel Parham, "Don't Cancel the Classics, Broaden and Diversify Them," May, 20, 2022, https://www.wsj.com/articles /dont-cancel-the-classics-broaden-and-diversify-them-education-college-charter-school -choice-systemic-racism-diversity-and-inclusion-clt-crt-ancients-greece-rome-homer -toni-morrison-11653079858.

was an issue for the people of Miletus. And their worries were not misguided. The silt from the Maeander River did eventually cover the entire bay of the town, and today Miletus is located five miles inland away from the sea.

What makes Thales such an important person, and the father of modern science and philosophy, is that he decided to describe the events around him and the problems caused by the Maeander River in a way that we today call scientific. He looked at causes and natural occurrences. He did not blame the gods or look to Greek mythology for an answer. And he used this scientific attitude to describe everything in the world around him. It might seem like a simple thing for us. But later ancient Greeks recognized Thales as the first one to have this attitude.

So what does this have to do with classical Catholic education? The common experience of high school students is that they go through their day taking a variety of classes that have nothing to do with each other. First-period math has nothing to do with the music elective at sixth period, and the third-period science class has nothing to do with gym or English Language Arts. The typical high school day is experienced as seven or eight independent and unrelated units. This experience is not healthy, and it is not true. The impulse of our curiosity to learn and to know should be one united movement toward interrelated aspects of the one truth of the world. Everything we learn in school is connected. There is math in music and music in math. There is science in history and a history to science. All of the subjects that are studied throughout the day are connected. But the connections are rarely emphasized, leading to an implied experience of different truths. But the truth of creation shows that everything about us and our world is connected. There is one truth. And this truth leads us to an encounter with the one who is Truth itself.

And this is why Thales of Miletus is such an important figure. After all, his intellectual curiosity and investigation eventually led to all the different areas that get studied in a normal high school day. But for him, all these fields were not different areas of study but one catalyst to discover the truth. Science and philosophy and music and literature and math and art and language and psychology and history were all related for Thales. And high schools do a great disservice when they fail to show their students how all the different subjects are aspects of the one truth that we are seeking, the one knowledge that helps us understand who we are and why we are here on this planet. And when the different disciplines show us how they are all connected and point to the one truth of the universe and human existence, it becomes much easier to realize how the truth of the world can lead us back to the author of all truth, who is often named Truth and Wisdom. Thales reminds us that all learning is connected. And this understanding is central in classical Catholic education.

THE TRANSCENDENTALS

One of the many contributions of the Greek philosophical tradition is the development of the discourse around being. The fact that things exist, that they have "being," might seem painfully obvious and unworthy of discussion. But the dialogue about being is one of the most powerful conversations that has taken place in Western civilization, and this discussion is the topic of metaphysics, the study of reality and being. Metaphysics is the ultimate example of meta-awareness. And that which all being has in common is that it is true, beautiful, and good.

Plato, in the dialogue *Phaedrus*, has his hero, Socrates, speculate about the nature of the soul. Using a parable that matches the Allegory of the Cave in its strength and beauty, Socrates likens the human person to a chariot pulled by winged horses. The ultimate goal is to ascend to the realm of beauty and goodness. This discussion has all the important elements of Plato's view of reality: that there is a reality more real than the present world, a reality of pure being where things exist in their ultimate form with ultimate truth and ultimate beauty. For Plato, our task in life is to remember the truth and beauty of this ideal world so that we might be informed of this ultimate reality and transform our present condition into one of greater purpose but also greater happiness. This is the life of one who has left the cave, one who allows their winged horses to pull together and raise them back up to heaven, to the vision of ultimate reality that was lost but must be remembered. For Plato, this recollection is the essence of education.

> [I speak of] him who, when he sees the beauty of earth, is transported with the recollection of the true beauty; he would like to fly away, but he cannot; he is like a bird fluttering and looking upward and careless of the world below. . . . For, as has been already said, every soul of man has in the way of nature beheld true being.[2]

St. Thomas Aquinas is one of the greatest theologians the Church has ever produced. Living in the thirteenth century, this Dominican friar explored all aspects of Catholic theology and connected them with the thinking of the ancient sages of Greece and Rome, primarily Plato and Aristotle. He is famous for his work the *Summa theologiae*, which is a summary and commentary on most points of Catholic theology.

Thomas expounds on truth, beauty, and goodness as the fundamental aspects of all reality, an idea described by Plato and Aristotle. Called "the transcendentals," these characteristics are the aspects of being that are common to all things and transcend any particular classification. By virtue of a thing's existence, it has a certain rationality, a truth, that can be understood and communicated. The reality of the thing has a certain harmony and proportion that makes it beautiful, and therefore also desirable

2. Plato, *Phaedrus*, in *The Dialogues of Plato*, vol. 1, trans. Benjamin Jowett (New York: Charles Scribner, 1871), 583–584.

and good. These aspects of reality all point to and find their origin and fulfillment in the first cause of being, the Prime Mover, God.

This metaphysical sensibility is perhaps the most fundamental aspect of classical education and points to the greatest difference and greatest strength of classical Catholic education. What is the point of high school? Regardless of what people think they should answer to this question, most parents approach high school with a practical attitude of "Where will my child go to college?" or "Will they be able to get a job?" These are important questions. However, job training is only one aspect of what education should provide our children. And, ultimately, we are not defined by our career or our jobs but by who we are as people.

When meeting parents for the first time, I usually ask them to sit down. Once they are comfortable and prepared, I tell them that I am not interested in getting their child ready for college. And I honestly mean that. Even if they do not realize it, most parents are driven by the next immediate goal for their child. But there is no way that I would feel a sense of vocation about spending four years getting people ready for four more years of education or for a job, or even a career. I have too much respect for my students to limit them to such a small part of their lives. My focus is to help them to develop a metaphysical view of the world, to see the truth, the goodness, and the beauty of themselves and the created space around them. They need to understand that evil, ugliness, and sin are not part of God's creation but the absence of the creative power and beauty that he intended and distortions of reality, sometimes of our own making. Whatever job my students may one day have, or whether they become spouses, or religious, or parents, or unemployed, or underemployed, or successful, or depressed, or content—all these things are just a part of the reality that is the most real, the reality of being be-ings. This means seeing themselves and the world around them through the eyes of the author of all reality, the one who loved us into existence, gives us being at every moment, and looks at us and sees that we are good—very good. I will not let my students define themselves by a college acceptance letter, a job, an illness, monetary success, or anything other than the love of their Father.

Ironically, by taking the focus away from a small goal like standardized tests or college acceptance, or even work, students are free to embrace the call to excellence that is implicit in a metaphysical understanding of the world. Throughout all the tragedy and joy of life, they are called to a life of flourishing, what Aristotle named *eudaimonia*. This call remains the same for us. There is nothing less practical and yet more important than philosophy and metaphysics. It will change the lives of students and give them a new understanding of existence and freedom, like one who has escaped from chains in a cave into the sunlight. Since this philosophical worldview is also inherent in the way the Church understands herself and explains divine revelation, it enables students to think with the mind of the Church. This is the essence of classical Catholic education, and it is awesome.

SOCRATIC SEMINAR: MENO'S SLAVE

It is a well-known fact of history that Socrates was not a handsome man. Multiple authors, on several occasions, mention his pug nose, bulging eyes, and lack of care about his dress and personal hygiene. If his appearance made an impression, it was not for the right reasons. But the Athenians were much more impacted by their interactions with the shabby sage, with his sharp debating style and penetrating insights. The method of asking deeper and deeper questions about a topic and not being satisfied with fancy but indeterminate answers is the greatest legacy of the Athenian philosopher. It was something that he employed throughout his life and that gave birth to the dialogue format in the writings of his student Plato. In one of these dialogues, Plato even gives a concrete lesson for why and how to apply this teaching method.

In one of the earliest written dialogues, Plato has his mentor Socrates discussing the acquisition of virtue with the young, ambitious military commander Meno. At one point, Socrates asserts that learning is a process of remembering. Believing that we are reincarnated souls, he says our goal in education is to force ourselves to remember our experiences from the world of forms where we existed before becoming incarnate. In that world, everything exists in its perfect state. To illustrate his point, he poses a series of questions to a young slave. Uneducated, the boy is able to perform a geometric proof with the guidance of Socrates. Through a series of questions by the old man, the young slave acquires new understanding and insight. In the mind of Socrates and Plato, however, he is merely recalling the truth that he knew prior to birth.

This example has provided a framework for a pedagogical approach known as the Socratic seminar, in which the teacher acts as a guide and mentor, possibly even a midwife, while students learn by asking deeper and deeper questions about a text, a concept, a teaching, etc. When done correctly, this format provides a vibrant and dynamic learning environment where students are not only engaged and active but excited about new learning. Although the teacher always has a goal in mind about where the discussion should land and what important points need to be covered, the path to getting there is unique and different with every class. I have taught some of the same material for over twenty years and had a different conversation on every occasion. I have learned something new in every discussion. It is a powerful and engaging teaching method. It allows for differentiation and close monitoring of the knowledge acquisition process. At every moment, through body language and eye contact, I can make continual assessments of where each student is with achieving mastery with the material. I can ask students with an emerging sense of mastery to explain a part of the material for someone who is somewhat confused, allowing both to grow in their understanding. Those who have mastered the concept can make associations and applications to other material that illustrate and explain the idea in a new and perhaps better way for some of their classmates. It is a dynamic and vibrant pedagogical method.

But there is one other benefit of class discussion that I did not initially expect but have come to appreciate as its most important aspect: seminar gives students a voice. And the whole structure of the seminar implicitly informs the student that what they say matters. At a time in their life where they suffer from near-chronic insecurity and a sense of powerlessness in the face of relentless change, Socratic discussion reaffirms their importance at a very deep level. This is subtle and unspoken, but it has an enormous impact on the personal well-being of the student. It also speaks to differentiated learning. In the seminar, all contributions are valuable. They are not all correct—this is not an opinion party. Our discussions are always connected to a text, and the students need to substantiate their claims with citations. There can be varied interpretations, and there often are. But it is a search for truth, and, just as with Socrates, wrong answers are sometimes the best way to arrive at a true understanding of the text. Add to the mix a little training in empathy and a reminder to work hard to understand the thoughts of others, and you get a classroom experience that is electric and electrifying.

THE CHURCH AS GUIDE: ST. CLEMENT OF ROME

Classical Catholic education is rooted in the person of Christ and his Church. The journey of education and self-discovery, if it is to lead to eternal life, is one that is guided by the Catholic faith and the grace of the Catholic Church. This reinforces the reality that the intellectual journey of education finds a beautiful complement in the lived experience of the pilgrim people of God. The encounter with truth within the classroom finds an emotional strengthening and underpinning by embarking on an actual pilgrimage, a voyage of spiritual or historical significance. This journey becomes an opportunity for integration that unites the learned material with a lived encounter in an experiential and personal way. In anticipation of the great jubilee of 2000, the Church addressed the importance of pilgrimage in our journey of faith, stating, "In pilgrimages, people acknowledge that 'from the very circumstances of his origin, man is . . . invited to converse with God,' and therefore through this, he is helped to discover that the way he is offered, to 'remain in intimate union with God,' is Christ, the Word made flesh. . . . In their totality, pilgrimages must show 'that for human beings, the Creator is not an anonymous and remote power; He is the Father,' and we are all his children, brothers and sisters in Christ the Lord."[3]

But, as *Brideshead* illustrates, the spiritual journey is not always easy. It is a sad reality of today's society that many Catholics are losing their faith. In examining this sobering truth, it is important to identify when and why people reject the faith. According to a Pew Research report, 79% of those leaving the Church do so before the age of twenty-three.[4] A majority say that their loss of faith arose from a lack of belief in the Church's teaching and because their spiritual needs were not being met.[5] Catholic education helps to stem the tide to a certain extent. Comparing students from Catholic schools to those in public education, 36% of those attending Catholic school still practiced the faith as compared to 25% with a public school background. Additionally, 41% of those who attended Catholic school still identified as Catholic and practiced occasionally as compared to 44% from public schools. Although the difference between Catholic and public education is significant, the overall statistics are alarming.[6] Neither 36% nor 25% are encouraging numbers.

3. Pontifical Council for the Pastoral Care of Migrants and Itinerant People, *The Pilgrimage in the Great Jubilee* (Boston: Pauline Books & Media, 1998), 33.

4. Brandon Vogt, "New Stats on Why Young People Leave the Church," https://brandonvogt.com/new-stats-young-people-leave-church/.

5. Vogt, "New Stats."

6. Brendan Hodge, "Special Report: Why Catholics Leave; Why Catholics Stay," The Pillar, November 9, 2021, https://www.pillarcatholic.com/special-report-why-catholics-leave/.

In part, these statistics might account for the tremendous growth in classical Catholic education in the past years. The metaphysical and integral worldview that are essential hallmarks of classical education are markedly different from contemporary Common Core education, which is used near-universally in non-classical Catholic schools. This creates a certain tension for non-classical Catholic schools that, through Common Core standards, have a utilitarian emphasis in their pedagogy and educational purpose while trying to uphold the Church's understanding of the human person in their Catholic identity. This tension does not exist in classical Catholic schools. This is because the philosophical foundation, theological teaching, and educational pedagogy of the Catholic Church throughout the ages is consistent with today's revival of classical Catholic education. As one classical Catholic teacher put it, "The Church's vision for education is classical."[7] And this has been so since the Church's beginning.

The First Letter of St. Clement, Bishop of Rome, to the Church in Corinth is one of the oldest Church documents. Pope Clement was third to succeed St. Peter the Apostle. His pontificate was during the first century, and what is fascinating is that John the Apostle was still alive. Corinth was a harbor city in Greece with a fledgling Church community started by St. Paul himself. When they experienced a tumultuous break within their local Church, the community turned to Clement of Rome and not John the Apostle. This alludes to the importance of the Bishop of Rome in the early Church. The situation was started by a group of upstart, overly confident young men (I like to think they were teenage boys!) who refused to listen to the elders. The community appealed to Clement, who graciously but firmly reminded them that they needed to adopt a spirit of humility. Clement starts

---

7. Denver Catholic Staff, "Going Crazy for Classical Education," Denver Catholic, March 10, 2017, https://denvercatholic.org/going-crazy-classical-education/.

off by apologizing for his delayed response because life has been so hectic. "Owing, dear brethren, to the sudden and successive calamitous events which have happened to ourselves, we feel that we have been somewhat tardy in turning our attention to the points respecting which you consulted us; and especially to that shameful and detestable sedition, utterly abhorrent to the elect of God, which a few rash and self-confident persons have kindled to such a pitch of frenzy, that your venerable and illustrious name, worthy to be universally loved, has suffered grievous injury."[8]

After a lengthy exposition that draws heavily from both the Old and New Testaments (parts of which had still to be written!), Clement exhorts the troublemakers to stop causing division within the community. "You therefore, who laid the foundation of this sedition, submit yourselves to the presbyters, and receive correction so as to repent, bending the knees of your hearts."[9] With these words and others like them, the authority of the Bishop of Rome is clearly on display. As such, the letter offers beautiful and extremely early insight into the nature of the Church and reflects many of the important teachings concerning ecclesiology in the *Catechism of the Catholic Church*.

There is a church in Rome built in honor of St. Clement. On the back wall, in the apse, there is a beautiful mosaic that illustrates the unity of the Church by depicting various members of the communion of saints connected by an ornate vine that stems from the cross in the center of the mosaic. The crucifix is portrayed as the tree of life, hearkening back to the garden of paradise as well as the metaphor of the tree in the first Psalm. The mosaic, which includes various figures such as farmers, shepherds, saints, and various animals, brings to life the passage in St. John's Gospel: "I am the vine, you are the branches. Those who abide in me and

8. Clement of Rome, *The First Epistle of Clement to the Corinthians*, trans. John Keith, Ante-Nicene Fathers, vol. 9, ed. Allan Menzies (Buffalo, NY: Christian Literature, 1896), newadvent.org.
9. Clement, *First Epistle*.

I in them bear much fruit, because apart from me you can do nothing" (John 15:5). Every year, I attempt to bring my students on a pilgrimage to Rome and to the Basilica of St. Clement after having read his epistle in class. Standing in that ancient and holy place, our membership in the communion of saints, our connection to believers from all times and all places, becomes a perceptible and unmistakable reality, while the admonition of St. Clement rings in our ears: "Let your children be partakers of true Christian training; let them learn of how great avail humility is with God—how much the spirit of pure affection can prevail with him—how excellent and great his fear is, and how it saves all those who walk in it with a pure mind."[10]

Personal Reflection from a College Student: Dora

I clearly remember one theology class junior year in which we had a conversation about this relationship between faith and reason. My teacher stopped me in my tracks when he said something I remember to this day: you can't blindly give yourself to faith. It is the best possible thing to seek to understand this faith and God with all that you are.

As a student in the Catholic parochial school system since the age of two, I'd long known how to rattle off the works of mercy or name the Beatitudes. I'd been taught what "we believe," and I'd learned that the tenets in our glossy new paperback textbooks, which I had picked up and read thoroughly, were all I had to do to be a good Catholic. This model of religious education, although it was taught by kind, well-intentioned teachers, still lacked something I could never then have put my finger on.

What was it that I didn't learn—or understand? Who God was, why I was supposed to follow him, and whether I could ever

---

10. Clement, *First Epistle*.

truly experience his influence? All that I knew was a simplistic but confusing how.

This changed in high school when I entered a classical program within my archdiocesan school called the Chesterton Scholars Program, or CSP for short. Catholic schooling taught me what to do—but classical Catholic schooling taught me who I was doing it for, and why.

The first time we read Plato's *Republic*, early in my freshman year, this happened with a question. How can this pagan text help to lead us to some deeper understanding of some eternal truth? As my classmates and I conversed in the seminar-style classroom, I realized something I had never realized in a class before. Every one of these fourteen-year-olds was striving, in some way, to ask the same question. What is truth? It was the same question that Socrates pursued, the same question Aristotle tackled. Instead of sitting around desks, teaching ourselves by rote memorization (as I had come to expect), we were attempting to answer the eternal questions of humanity. We students were doing it poorly, but we were doing it—guided by a careful, deliberate hand, constantly rooted (in philosophy or theology) in the Catholic faith.

St. Augustine's *Confessions* opened sophomore year. Until high school, my religious education seemed to presume that every child placed in "religion" class had already had, or would have, a spontaneous conversion of heart. Being a skeptical, curious child, I was not convinced by this. I understood, perhaps, that there was a God. But what could this Unknown really do to me? Right around sophomore year, this lack of knowledge began to terrify me. I wondered if this God my family and school life had been centered on was simply used to control my Sunday mornings, or worse still, that he was accessible to others but inaccessible to me. And then, in CSP Literature, I encountered Augustine. A saint who I related to on an entirely new level: a saint who first had to understand the idea of God using the light of reason before he could give himself fully to God. Augustine gave me hope. And I began to understand why.

Then came St. Thomas Aquinas, junior year. When we finally tackled the bear of the *Summa theologiae*, I felt prepared. We had read texts from Homer to Chaucer to Spinoza, encountered various views on truth, discussed and dissected them all. I could do the same for this, surely. I was not, however, prepared for the "take up and read" that the *Summa* would become for me. Aquinas' dense prose contained truths about God and about virtue that I had never come close to considering. Aquinas attempted to offer real replies to the questions I'd had all along, marrying the philosophy of ancient Greece with the Church to display God's glory. Aquinas seemed to have it all. I finally understood, through reading the *Summa* in CSP theology, what it could be like to know the faith—to know the God I was striving to believe in.

Where does classical Catholic education come into the spiritual journey I've described? My answer is this: I would not have done any of what I've described without classical education. I would never have reached the level of informed curiosity that allowed me to "take up and read." I would never have been able to identify the goodness of God that emerges throughout human history. The classical canon, illuminated by salvation history, offers a glimpse into the trajectory of humanity afforded by no glossy textbook. With the human question—the search for eternal truth—guiding the reading of these timeless writings, the incarnate God can be seen in between the lines. Achilles' valiant plea for honor is clearly empty, Aristotle's definition of virtue incomplete, without Christ. Without classical education, I would have never read these texts. Without classical Catholic education, I would have never witnessed the truths of God and humanity they contain.

I'm now a freshman in college. My friends and I have not shied away from those discussions that were before reserved to the classroom, and one question that has occupied many hours this year is this: What is the best way to educate the child? My answer will always be: the method of classical education I received in the Chesterton Scholars Program. Because of its classical model, I find myself deeply grounded in the Catholic faith and able to engage in good-natured, informed dialogue with my highly intelligent peers, purely because of the model of classical Catholic education that formed me for four years. I've found that intellectual conversion is not just for Augustine, and philosophy is not just for the Greeks. Classical learning is for everyone—and when that classical learning is directed toward the eternal truth, all roads lead to Christ.

CONCLUSION

Classical education predates the coming of Christ. It provided its students with those skills and areas of knowledge that the ancient world believed one needed to possess in order to be an engaged member of society. These arts needed by a free member of society were grouped together into the seven liberal arts. Today, in an analogous way, the liberal arts, as opposed to vocational training, help us to become an educated member of the world around us with a valuable contribution that only we can add. In the process, we discover who we are and how we can flourish in this life. It is not job training, but life training. Regardless of what our many jobs or careers might be, whether we are successful in our careers or chronically underemployed, or how happy or challenging our home and personal life end up being, education with a classical Catholic pedagogy will help orient students toward that which is true, good, and beautiful. Ultimately, it will help students learn to see themselves as children of God, unconditionally loved by the Father, and called to be heirs to the heavenly kingdom and members of his Church.

Not a bad way to spend the four years of high school.

PART II

Discovering Christ
in the Classroom

What Happens in the Classroom?

After discussing the various essential elements of a classical Catholic education, it is illustrative to see what happens within a classical classroom to give parents and educators a sense of the unity and scope of the learning experience. A classical curriculum will apply these various aspects of pedagogy, integrate the various fields of study covered by the liberal arts, and highlight the unifying and narrative elements already present in our history.

There is a narrative arc to salvation history. After the fall, God promised redemption and laid out his plan to bring forgiveness and blessing to the world through his relationship with Abraham. In the fullness of time, God sent his Son to redeem us. But this incarnation of God within humanity also changed how we understand ourselves. Civilization and culture could not remain the same after this divine revelation. The centuries since the birth of Christ have witnessed great strides in integrating faith and reason, spirituality and daily life. But in the modern era, humanity has also increasingly rejected God's understanding of the human person and attempted to define itself apart from God. Today, just as in every time before us, we must make a conscious choice to believe in God and follow his commands. This is the drama of human history.

The fourth chapter will explore the learning and culture of the ancient world. The period of human history before the birth of Christ is a time marked by a sense of longing. In literature and philosophy, in the events of human history, and in the revelation of God to the Hebrew people, we see a sense of anticipation. The world longed for redemption and unification with our heavenly Father.

The fact that the second person of the Trinity, the Son of God, became man at a certain time and a certain place in history is mind-boggling. When I'm studying the Old Testament with students, they often ask why Jesus did not come sooner with less preparation and anticipation. After years of studying and teaching Scripture, however, I am usually left with the exact opposite question: How could humanity ever be ready to embrace God as one of their own? It is staggering to think of the overwhelming love of God that the life and death of Jesus Christ reveal to us.

The fifth chapter explores the impact of the Incarnation on the human story. And this event, this truth, changes everything about human history and our understanding of ourselves and the world around us. It provides us with a totally new view of the human story and the human person. In *Gaudium et Spes*, the fathers of the Second Vatican Council wrote, "The truth is that only in the mystery of the incarnate Word does the mystery of man take on light. . . . By the revelation of the mystery of the Father and His love, [Christ] fully reveals man to man himself and makes his supreme calling clear."[1] This understanding of the human person is called Christian anthropology, and it teaches us that we have a dignity and a calling beyond anything we could ever imagine for ourselves. Since the whole story of humanity, as well as our own personal history, is defined by our response to God's invitation for a loving relationship, there can only be two ways of viewing the human person: through Christ, or through rejecting God and looking to ourselves to define our humanity. These

---

1. Second Vatican Council, *Gaudium et Spes* 22, pastoral constitution, December 7, 1965, vatican.va.

two anthropologies, the Christian and the secular, summarize the human story and provide the narrative arcs for a robust and integrated classical Catholic curriculum.

The sixth chapter focuses on the period of the High Middle Ages when Catholic culture was at its most fully integrated. This period is often ignored or looked at condescendingly since the modern eye cannot appreciate the great harmony that existed within society between love of God and neighbor. However, this age of Christian culture, known as Christendom, is the true Age of Enlightenment, and it produced hospitals, schools, universities, and countless other advances that we consider the hallmarks of civilized society.

The seventh chapter chronicles the growth of the secular humanist worldview that is ever more prevalent in the modern world. Secular anthropology was first born in the Garden of Eden when Adam and Eve turned their backs on God. It was the cunning serpent that led them astray by planting seeds of doubt. These same seeds were planted in the history of philosophy. In his *Meditations on First Philosophy*, René Descartes introduces the category of doubt as an existential approach to reality. Through skepticism, Descartes was able to mistrust everything exterior to himself and experience himself as an isolated center of consciousness. Doubt replaced hope, the human "I" replaced the divine "I Am," and secular anthropology replaced Christian anthropology.

This is the human drama, and this arc provides the content and narrative flow for classical Catholic education. When we focus on the story of one particular period and look at all subjects from that vantage point, the human story provides us with a way to unite all the learning that happens within a given year. We will see examples of how this can be effectively done in the next four chapters. Each chapter is an example of a horizontal arc in education, where you connect all the subject material in a given year to a given historical time period and/or theme. As this horizontal arc is built over the years, the impact is compounded as the historical narrative unfolds into a vertical edifice that connects truth from various years and subjects, building a firm foundation of learning and personal growth. In fact, the presence of ever-increasing vertical arcs within a curriculum provides a symphonic and exponential impact to education that is both compelling and transformative for the student.

In addition to providing the unifying narrative and overarching arc, this cadence of classical pedagogy also provides the template for how students learn. This model of curiosity, understanding, and mastery even reaches the level of the individual lesson plan. Dr. Eric DeMeuse, Headmaster of the Chesterton Academy of Milwaukee, has done important work in highlighting the stages of an individual lesson plan to align with the four key periods of salvation history used in the second part of this book: anticipation, incarnation, culmination, application. This unites the classical pedagogy known as mimetic instruction with the cadence of God's relationship with humanity. First, you must help the students understand why the material is important to them. Why should they care? Help awaken a sense of longing. Then, help the students give birth to the idea or concept. Culmination takes place when mastery is achieved and the students have fully integrated the new learning. Proof of this mastery can be found in the application to other analogous or unique scenarios. This model combines the rhythm of salvation history with the core aspects of classical pedagogy.

The following chapters will provide examples of how these horizontal arcs are built throughout the study of each of these time periods and how vertical arcs emerge when the various aspects of education are integrated and combined together as one revelatory narrative. At the same time, while highlighting these horizontal and vertical arcs, key aspects of classical instruction and the liberal arts will also be discussed. By thus focusing on the truth of the human person as revealed by God, we can create environments that allow students to discover the love of Christ in the classroom.

4

The Ancient World

Longing for Christ

SEARCHING FOR AN ANSWER TO A QUESTION YOU DIDN'T KNOW YOU HAD

"Sing, O goddess, the anger of Achilles . . ." The *Iliad* is one of the first and greatest texts of Western civilization. When asked, most people say that it is the story of the Trojan War and the famous Trojan horse. But that is not the story of the *Iliad*. There is no Trojan horse, and, although set against the backdrop of the famous conflict between the Greeks and Trojans, this epic poem is not about the war that rages on the battlefield. Rather, it is the story of one man named Achilles, of his battle with the rage that consumes him, and of his journey to find a love that will conquer this anger.

The story begins with the leader of the Greek army, Agamemnon, who is forced to return his concubine to appease the gods. Humiliated, Agamemnon lashes out. His greatest warrior, Achilles, tells the general to accept the will of the gods and focus on the riches that will be his when they successfully defeat Troy. Instead, Agamemnon directs his anger at Achilles, and the two enter into a quickly escalating argument, one that would have turned fatal for Agamemnon if the goddess Athena did not intervene and stay the hand of Achilles. Enraged and humiliated, Achilles vows to no longer fight for the Greeks and returns to his tent to sit out the war.

Throughout the rest of the poem, Achilles is left to deal with his violent anger, an anger that consumes him and robs him of his peace. There is nothing that can help him overcome his rage. His attempt to find comfort in *eros*, sexual love, fails. And his love of friends, what the Greeks called *philia*, only makes his anger grow stronger. His inability to find peace even leads to a set of events that ends with the death of his dearest friend, Patroclus.[1]

By this point in the story, Achilles is a man completely possessed by anger. He rages against everyone: the Greeks, the Trojans, and the world around him. In his blind rage, he even attacks the river. It is at this point that the king of the Trojans, Priam, the enemy of the Greeks, sends his greatest and most noble warrior, his most beloved son, Hector, to fight, one on one, against Achilles. But Priam knows that his son will die. Hector, too, knows that he will die at the hands of Achilles. Everyone, even Hector's infant son, knows that this man, this blameless and noble son, will die at the hands of Achilles.

The *Iliad* culminates in the final book, book 24, not with a Trojan horse or the fall of Troy but with King Priam slipping behind enemy lines to beg Achilles for the body of his dead child. Unconcerned about his pride or even his life, the king falls on his knees and begs the man who murdered his son to give him back the body of Hector. As Priam weeps and begs for Hector's body, Achilles is touched by the love of this father and by his sacrifice. For a brief moment, his heart melts, tears come to his eyes, and his anger abates. Achilles gives Priam the incorrupt body of his son.

The final scene of the *Iliad* is a funeral banquet for Hector. This Greek poem, written for the Greek people eight hundred years before the advent of Christianity, ends with the burial ceremony of the beaten Trojan hero Hector. His incorrupt body is laid on wood and consumed by fire. Wine is poured over the remains, and his white bones are collected and put in a golden urn, which is buried and covered with stones. They set guards to watch the

1. The distinctions in the meaning of the word 'love' and the various Greek terms will be discussed again in chapter 7. For a more complete exposition, see C.S. Lewis, *The Four Loves*.

remains, and the final lines describe the banquet held in honor of this beloved son—the one sent to die for the sins of others and whose death quenched the burning anger that trapped Achilles.

> Forthwith they yoked their oxen and mules and gathered together before the city. Nine days long did they bring in great heaps of wood, and on the morning of the tenth day with many tears they took brave Hector forth, laid his dead body upon the summit of the pile, and set the fire thereto. Then when the child of morning, rosy-fingered dawn, appeared on the eleventh day, the people again assembled, round the pyre of mighty Hector. When they were got together, they first quenched the fire with wine wherever it was burning, and then his brothers and comrades with many a bitter tear gathered his white bones, wrapped them in soft robes of purple, and laid them in a golden urn, which they placed in a grave and covered over with large stones set close together. Then they built a barrow hurriedly over it keeping guard on every side lest the Achaeans should attack them before they had finished. When they had heaped up the barrow they went back again into the city, and being well assembled they held high feast in the house of Priam their king.
>
> Thus, then, did they celebrate the funeral of Hector tamer of horses.[2]

In his poem, Homer expresses the longing of the Greeks and the people of the ancient world. A longing for something more. For something greater. A longing for a love that they did not know or understand. One that would sacrifice everything. A longing for

2. Homer, *The Iliad*, 2nd ed., trans. Samuel Butler (Louisville, KY: Memoria, 2021), 446–447.

a beloved son sent by the Father to die for our sins. A love that would bring them peace.[3]

DISCOVERING GOD

Two hundred years after Homer sang of the sacrifice of Hector, Thales of Miletus began his search for natural explanations to the seemingly random changes that permeated daily reality. The conversation that this trailblazer started continued for hundreds of years among the Greeks and then from there for hundreds of years more all the way down to our time. It led to many scientific and mathematical discoveries. It influenced poetry and literature and gave rise to what we call philosophy. And it led to the discovery of God.

That might be an odd thing to say. After all, the Greeks already had gods—plenty of them—long before Thales came along. And one of the significant contributions of Thales was to describe the world by its own laws, without divine intervention. He started a conversation about the fundamental truth of the world. What was the essence of the universe, the thing that caused things to stay the same even if they went through enormous change? How can I grow taller, older, wiser, and balder over the years and yet stay the same person? How come a tree goes through so much change every year and yet stays that same tree? What makes a thing *this* thing and keeps it from becoming some other thing? These questions led to answers through science, but also through philosophy. Earlier,

3. The *Iliad* is a very challenging and complex work, well beyond the normal high school level. It is our job as classical educators to make the work accessible for the students through guided reading and class discussion. It is important to emphasize certain central themes and key moments in the narrative. For example, I focus on the final book and highlight those chapters and sections from previous books that explain the action at the end. When Priam falls at the knees of Achilles, he embraces him in a very odd way, but the same gesture is used in book 1 when Achilles' mother, Thetis, embraces Zeus. We often reenact this first instance so that it is well-known when it returns at the end of the poem. By allowing the story to explain all the important aspects of book 24 before reading it, the class can read straight through this moving scene without having to stop and interrupt the drama. The students are usually surprised by the Christological and Eucharistic overtones of the last pages of the *Iliad*.

I spoke about the importance of meta-awareness in education as a tool to teach students so that they can understand the deeper meanings and underlying connections to the world around them. And one way to help build this meta-awareness is by studying metaphysics.

There are several branches of study in philosophy. Metaphysics is the branch of philosophy that studies that which is beyond (or perhaps underneath) the physical world. This does not immediately mean the study of spiritual things. There are many things beyond the physical that are not strictly spiritual, such as the nature of a thing. Questions about love or friendship or beauty are examples. Or questions about what the essence of anything actually is. And even though Thales started the conversation for the ancient Greeks, Plato and Aristotle provided the most important answers.

Both of these men were giants in the world of thinking and understanding. They wrote answers to questions about the essence of love and friendship and beauty. They wrote observations about the physical world, governments and politics, and the underlying causes of reality. And as they wrote, and thought, and taught (because both men started what we would today call universities), they discovered something amazing about the world: that it must have been created by an all-powerful, never-changing being. And this being they called God.

Although Plato was very influential in formulating this discussion, it was Aristotle who developed the notion of the Prime Mover. This happened as a result of a dilemma that arose in the philosophical discussion of ancient Greece. Philosophers spent a lot of their time responding to previous philosophers as well as putting out their own thoughts and theories. A man named Parmenides came along in 500 BC and taught that change is impossible, that if something is, then it is, and it can never not be. Change is just an illusion. Existing is the most fundamental thing in reality and can not be divided into pieces. Or, to put it in an even more confusing way that philosophy teachers like to use on their students, a being's be-ing is the most fundamental being of that being.

This stumped the philosophical world for the next hundred years and caused philosophers to focus more on science than on metaphysics. And then Aristotle came along. He realized that a distinction needed to be made between the essential aspects of a thing that do not change, which are called the substance ("the thing that stands under"), and the characteristics that can or do change, which are known as the accidents. This is not the same thing as the normal use of the English word 'accident,' which means "an unexpected event." Something like the size, color, or location of a thing are accidental qualities. I cannot help but feel that the history of our nation would have been more just and equitable to all people if everyone had a better grasp of the difference between substance and accidents. After all, our color might be important in terms of our experience, but fundamentally—substantially—our shared humanity is a universal quality that connects and unites us all equally. And this distinction between substance and accidents is so important that the Church uses it to explain Jesus' presence in the Eucharist with the term 'transubstantiation.'

The terms 'substance' and 'accident' do not only explain what makes up a thing; they also explain the different kinds of changes that happen in the world. This helped Aristotle formulate the notion of substantial and accidental change as well as the category of potentiality—and this led to an answer to the problem posed by Parmenides. But at the same time, while exploring the idea of change in the world, Aristotle realized that this type of change could not have gone on infinitely. On the contrary, Aristotle said that the existence of substantial change means that there must be a first being that set everything in motion. He stated that this change of events could not have infinite regress. It must have had a first cause. And this cause he called the First Mover.

This argument can be found in Aristotle's book called (unsurprisingly) the *Metaphysics*. As he develops this realization, he comes to understand that this first being that causes all other beings to exist must be the fullness of existence and reality; that it can have no defect or unrealized potential; that it must be one and indivisible (as Parmenides had said); and that it is eternal, good, and beautiful. Nothing could be more real than this Prime Mover and nothing more true. And, in a world that celebrated a plethora of gods, with gods for war, the moon, and fire, Aristotle realized that this being must be the one and only true God. Without knowing what he was looking for, Aristotle had found the ultimate answer to the universe and to our lives. He had found the answer to a question that he did not even know he had. He had found God.

Personal Reflection from a High School Senior: Peter

It's complicated. I guess that would be my answer if you asked me about my faith life.

I've always been Catholic, and I've always attended Catholic school. I believed in God when I was young, sort of. But growing up, we rarely made it to Mass on Sunday, and I can't say that I thought too much about the faith or had a relationship with God. I never prayed. It was really hard to see God as a loving Father. My dad has been absent for nearly all of my life, and when he was there, it wasn't always healthy. I didn't have a model for how to see God as a loving father. Like I said, it's been complicated.

That was where I was spiritually when I entered high school. Being part of a Catholic school, I was forced to think more about my faith. But I struggled believing that God was there. It was tough since you can't see him and I had never had one of those experiences of God where you can feel him like some people do. I had a lot of doubts about the faith. It was hard to conceptualize everything, and it didn't make sense to me. Seeing how other Catholics acted just made things worse. It didn't seem very Christ-like. It was tough not seeing the faith used in action and not knowing God myself. Eventually I was on the point of giving up on God.

Throughout my years of classical education, I kept reading the Bible, studying the faith in class, and attending the school Masses. But this didn't make it easier for me to build a relationship with God. In a sense, it got harder. I still never felt God in my life and that really started to bother me. I really wanted someone to prove to me that God existed. I don't see him, I don't feel him. How do I know he is there? "What if it's just all made up to make people feel better about life and death?" I was still full of doubts.

By junior year, my faith was hanging by a thread. Parts of the Church's teaching were still confusing. I have family members who are Christian but not Catholic, and I didn't have an answer for things they were saying against the faith. Additionally, some of the problems that I have had in my life come from my dad being absent. It caused a lot of struggles, and I would blame them on my dad being absent, and then I would blame God. "Why aren't you looking out for me? Why is this happening to me?"

Things started to change senior year. I remember learning about Aristotle's discovery of God one day in philosophy class. It made a lot of sense. As we discussed it, I was like, "Okay. We have proof that a god exists. But how do we know that it is our God? A God that loves us and cares for us?" Then we talked about what Aristotle had said about the Prime Mover and how this ultimate being had to be completely good. That really hit me. This pagan philosopher was describing our God. I didn't just have to believe it; I could see how someone could figure it out. Knowing that it made sense helped me to believe in other things the faith was saying. I started to think, "Maybe this is something that is possible."

And then, during my senior retreat, I had an experience of God's love. I remember thinking, "Wow. Finally. I finally have a relationship with you!" It was awesome. I started praying more, I would read the Bible and try to get to Mass. I was making an effort.

After the retreat, I started to go to Adoration, and I started to talk with our campus minister about forgiving people who have hurt me, especially my dad. Since then I've tried to forgive him for specific hurts from my past. I can feel myself letting go of that pain. I don't struggle with God being real anymore, but I still have doubts about parts of the faith. The idea of hell really bothers me. I was back to the idea, "Was it just something that people made up to get people to do the right thing?" But I definitely feel God in my life, and I recognize him now in my interactions with other people.

By being at a Catholic high school and participating in their classical program, there is a lot of support to keep growing my faith. I keep asking questions so that I can understand things better. I talk to my teachers and our priest here at school about my questions and doubts. They seem to understand my journey and have experienced a lot of the same things themselves. I also have great friends who support my spiritual growth. They have helped me a lot, and I try to help them. I try to notice God in our interactions and to be as holy as I can with them. I really love my friends. And I like to bring my struggles and doubts to prayer. Someone once told me that any conversation with God is a prayer, even if I have doubts or if I'm angry. Praying doesn't have to be a prayer. I spend time with God. Sometimes I'm angry with him. But I'm glad that we are talking now.

My faith journey isn't over, and, like I said, it's been pretty complicated. But I've encountered God, and I know that he loves me. And I'm surrounded by people who love me, who are proud of me, and who support my faith. I'm thankful for my time in high school and what people have done to help me discover God. I think my life would be very different if I hadn't been at a school where people cared about me and wanted me to encounter God's love. My journey of faith is not over, and I'm looking forward to growing my relationship with God in college. But knowing that I have God as a Father who loves me has changed everything. Maybe it's not really that complicated after all.

———

SMALLER ARCS

Highlighting the arc in philosophy from Thales, the first pre-Socratic, to Aristotle and his teaching on the Prime Mover is just one example of how to build a horizontal arc in curriculum. Rather than study several random people, teachers can highlight how Thales began something that Aristotle completed. The unity of that search as one developing dialogue, which in this case results in one of the most amazing examples of natural revelation, provides a narrative arc to the information that makes it easier for the student to master and internalize the new knowledge. It can even have a profound, transformative effect. These types of narrative arcs should be used for individual lesson plans and entire courses. The beauty of a fully integrated curriculum is that it will strive to do this horizontally, across the entire grade, and vertically, building from year to year, so that all of high school becomes one extensive conversation held over multiple periods a day and spanning all four years. This is an essential aspect of classical Catholic education.

Building these arcs, however, requires great patience and confidence on the part of the teacher. Rather than give students all the information and answer all the questions, the classical teacher is trained to allow students to sit with their *unknowing*. In today's educational environment, where answers are easily attainable and education is built around knowing the exact information to provide on a test, embracing this patient approach can be unnerving to the modern student and difficult for the teacher. But there is much fruit in wrestling and accepting our ignorance, as Socrates would say. It allows us to see how multilayered, integrated, and beautiful truth is.

A FAITHFUL SPOUSE

While the longing for redemption and reunion with a loving God can be glimpsed in the ancient world, there was no vocabulary to express this longing in clear language. They yearned for what they knew not. And as the impressive empires of the Greeks, Egyptians, Babylonians, Persians, and Romans fought amongst themselves over the centuries for control of the Mediterranean world and the area of the Fertile Crescent, there arose a small kingdom of people who had a divine election.

Nestled in the precarious position on the route between the great empire of Egypt and the many powers of Mesopotamia, the children of Jacob, the Israelites, declared themselves to have encountered the one true God, to have been chosen by him to bring blessing to all humanity, and to have his inspired revelation written on parchment and committed to heart. They were the chosen people, and they had encountered the living, loving God who had revealed himself and made a covenant with them. The history of these people is the history of God's covenant with humanity. And this relationship is so personal and intense that the Lord explains this covenant as a marriage. Throughout Scripture, from the first pages of Genesis to the last page of Revelation, it is the institution of marriage that is used to describe the type of relationship that God is seeking with his people.

God is not subtle about his views of the covenant as a marriage or of his people's idolatry as marital infidelity. Time and again, he has his prophets accuse the people of Israel of not following the commandments given as part of the covenant. Their idolatrous worship of the god Baal is like adultery in God's eyes. One of the most poignant examples of this can be found with the prophet Hosea. "When the LORD first spoke through Hosea, the LORD said to Hosea, 'Go, take for yourself a wife of whoredom and have children of whoredom, for the land commits great whoredom by forsaking the LORD'" (Hosea 1:2). To exemplify the infidelity of the people, God is instructing Hosea to marry a prostitute. God instructs the prophet to name two of his children "Not pitied" and "Not my people" to further illustrate his point (Hosea 1:6, 9). Like I said, God is not subtle.

But rather than divorce Israel for its infidelity, God renews his covenantal promise to them, promising to wash them clean and take them back. This is the great promise that awaits his people—a new and everlasting covenant. One that will never be broken and will wash the people clean of their sins. This is the promise to Israel.

> On that day, says the LORD, you will call me, "My husband," and no longer will you call me, "My Baal." For I will remove the names of the Baals from her mouth, and they shall be mentioned by name no more. I will make for you a covenant on that day with the wild animals, the birds of the air, and the creeping things of the ground; and I will abolish the bow, the sword, and war from the land; and I will make you lie down in safety. And I will take you for my wife forever; I will take you for my wife in righteousness and in justice, in steadfast love, and in mercy. I will take you for my wife in faithfulness; and you shall know the LORD. (Hosea 2:16–20)

Using the theme of covenant to unify and explain Scripture is another example of providing a narrative arc within the material, which helps the student unify and structure information. In this case, it also provides cohesion and unity to the collection of biblical books as well as a profound insight into our most important relationship.

THE LORD OF HISTORY

Immediately after the first sin, God indicates that he has a plan to restore us to his love. His promise to save us became more and more clear throughout the history of God's covenant with the Hebrew people in the Old Testament. With more detail, but still somewhat vaguely, he explains the outline of his plan to Abraham. God's agenda became clearer still as the people entered a covenant with God on Mount Sinai and when they eventually took possession of the Promised Land. The kingship of David is an important moment in understanding God's promise to redeem us through an anointed King, the Lion of Judah, the Root of David (Rev. 5:5). By the time of the prophets, the expectation of God's Messiah, who would come and write the covenant not on stone but on our hearts (Jer. 31:33), was clearly articulated.

But as he prepared a chosen people from which the Messiah would rise up, God was also preparing the world to receive this message and allow it to spread with relative peace and safety. From about thirty years before the birth of Christ until the end of the second century, the world experienced a great period of stability without great wars or conflict, which was unique in history. This was the age of the *Pax Romana*, the Roman Peace, when the empire of Rome ruled the Mediterranean world without much challenge from other peoples. This period of stability allowed for the Good News of Jesus Christ and his young Church to spread throughout the known world and form strong roots. And this age of peace was the result of a bitter feud that involved adultery, power grabs, divorce, sibling rivalry, delusions of being gods, and suicide. It was basically a made-for-TV movie, and it all culminates in the Battle of Actium.

The story revolves around the powerful and captivating figure of Cleopatra. The last ruler of Egypt before it became a Roman province, Cleopatra assumed power in 51 BC at the death of her father. Throughout her reign of more than twenty years, she was continually fighting against family members for control of the throne. Her first victory came after her brother was defeated by Julius Caesar at the Battle of the Nile in 47 BC. It is thought that Julius Caesar and Cleopatra had a love affair at this time that produced a son, Caesarion. She was in Rome visiting Caesar in 44 BC during his famous assassination. At this point, the story already seems as outlandish as a reality TV show.

Several years later, Cleopatra and Mark Antony, one of Julius Caesar's loyal companions and one of the new rulers of Rome, began a love affair of their own that lasted until Mark Antony's death in 30 BC. Initially, they were unable to marry because Mark Antony was married to Octavia Minor, the sister of another one of the rulers of Rome, Gaius Octavian. After ten years of romance and three children, Mark Antony and Cleopatra made their relationship official in an elaborate public ceremony in which they dressed themselves as two of the most important Egyptian gods. Shortly thereafter, Mark Antony divorced his wife Octavia and married Cleopatra. For this and other political reasons, Octavia's brother, Octavian, who was Julius Caesar's adopted son, began a campaign against Mark Antony. This culminated in the Battle of Actium, a naval battle between the forces of Octavian on the one side and the combined fleets of Mark Antony and Cleopatra on the other, which was fought in the waters near the Greek city of Actium in 31 BC.

Although Octavian had four hundred ships to Mark Antony's five hundred, the former's ships were smaller and faster and could do more damage. Octavian also benefited from the desertion of Mark Antony's general, who brought with him Mark Antony's battle plans. As the battle progressed on September 2, 31 BC, Mark Antony employed a time-tested strategy of engaging his opponent from one side while the forces of Cleopatra attacked Octavian's fleet from the other. This was usually a solid plan for victory, but not this time. Instead, as the battle continued to rage throughout the day, Cleopatra retreated with her ships to Egypt. Mark Antony, breaking through Octavian's line, followed her but lost much of his military forces in doing so.

The final battle between Octavian and Mark Antony took place the next year in Egypt. When victory seemed impossible and he received a false report that his beloved Cleopatra had died, Mark Antony stabbed himself. As he lay dying, he received an updated message that Cleopatra was actually still alive, after which, utterly defeated, he died. Upon hearing of the defeat and death of her lover, Cleopatra committed suicide. They were a real-life prototype of Romeo and Juliet.[4]

Octavian, the adopted son of Julius Caesar, was now the sole ruler of the Roman Empire, and with his ascendancy to power, the *Pax Romana* began. He took the name Caesar Augustus, and it is this ruler who is mentioned in the opening pages of Luke's Gospel (Luke 2:1–7).

In the chronicles of humanity, we see that God is the Lord of history. And throughout antiquity, he prepared the human family to receive his Son as one of their own. "But when the fullness of time had come, God sent his Son, born of a woman, born under the law, in order to redeem those who were under the law, so that we might receive adoption as children" (Gal. 4:4–5).

SUMMARY

Humanity of the ancient world yearned for something greater. This longing was described in the story of the *Odyssey*, where Homer beautifully writes about an earthly family, bound together by love and loyalty, striving to return to one another. This chapter also looked at Homer's other famous poem, which is one of the oldest stories of the Western canon, the *Iliad*. This ancient epic, from 800 BC, shows the longing within ancient humanity for someone who can redeem us from our pain, for a loving father who knowingly sends his son to die for the sins of others. In philosophy, this longing reached its clearest expression in the writings of the Greek sage Aristotle, who argued that the world must necessarily be created by an all-powerful being, a First Mover, whom he called God. These mental preparations for the birth of Jesus Christ, Truth

---

4. The late author Warren Carroll was unsurpassed in his ability to provide history in a dramatic and exciting way that was firmly grounded in the centrality of the Incarnation. See Warren H. Carroll, "The Winning of the Roman Peace," in *A History of Christendom*, vol. 1, *The Founding of Christendom* (Front Royal, VA: Christendom Press, 2004), for more on this time period, including the Battle of Actium.

incarnate, were paralleled by the preparations that God undertook in his revelations to the Hebrew people. The Lord's covenantal relationship with Israel is a marriage in God's eyes, and when his people forsake the Lord and the law of the covenant, God accuses the Israelites of committing adultery. This is apparent on almost every page of Scripture, but few illustrations are as jarring or obvious as the family of the prophet Hosea. God's plan is not only clear in the history of the Hebrew people but also outside of the country of Israel. Some of the wildest moments of military history in the ancient world bear the mark of divine preparation for the birth of the Son of God made man. These reflections show that Christ can be found in every aspect of the classroom—in literature, philosophy, and history, but also music, math, etc.—and that the ancient world was a time of longing for the coming of Christ.

The Incarnation

Christian Anthropology

IN YOUR EYES

I first experienced the love of God in high school. Even though I had been raised in the faith and attended Catholic schools with excellent teachers and good content, I had no idea who God was when I encountered him. I was not able to connect what I had learned with the reality of a heavenly Father whose love was overwhelming. That experience of God put me on a path of discovery. I needed to know who this loving person was and how to respond. So when I went to college, I signed up for a religion class on the Old Testament. It was awful. Rather than bringing me closer to God, I would leave the lectures wondering if the Bible was a fabrication. Plus, the class was boring. I went straight from my religion class to a biology class held in a giant auditorium. Unfortunately, the science teacher was openly hostile to any religious sentiment. He would mock any notion of the supernatural. But as I sat in his class, full of doubt from my religion class, in an environment that was hostile to the divine, I became overwhelmed by the beauty of God's creation. It was especially the study of the cell that convinced me of God's design in the universe. Walking back to my dorm, I was filled with a sense of God's existence and providence.[1] It was

---

1. There is a whole genre of literature that discusses the importance of faith and science. Some are specifically age-appropriate for high school students, such as *Brilliant! 25 Catholic Scientists, Mathematicians and Supersmart People* by David and Jaclyn Warren or the textbook *Faith, Science, and Reason* by Midwest Theological Forum. Other books work to prove faith through a lens of natural revelation with scientific data.

a rollercoaster of spiritual experiences where things I did to grow closer to God would fail, while other parts of my day, which tried to tear me from God, brought me deeper into his presence.

And this is why our goal as classical Catholic educators must be to create environments where students can encounter God's love—in the classroom, in the books we select and the way we teach them. And I am not speaking only about religion class. Teachers and administrators need to consciously work to reveal the beauty of God's love in every class. This is why the integrated approach of a classical environment is so consistent with creating these environments. The Catholic identity of a classical school really becomes apparent and meaningful to the students when it is present in every classroom, every club, and every activity. But, going back to my comments in chapter 1, all we can do is invite and encourage. We cannot choose a relationship with Christ for anyone; students must do it themselves. And high school students are dealing with a lot. There are many highs in high school, but there are also many traumas, insecurities, and anxieties.

"Truth exists. The Incarnation happened." This was the famous saying of Dr. Warren Carroll, the Catholic historian and founder of Christendom College. It is a pithy way to express several truths simultaneously: the importance of objective reality, the unity of truth, the connection between truth and the Incarnation, and the centrality of the Incarnation in our lives—spiritual, personal, and academic. But the Incarnation must happen within each of us. We must give birth to Christ in our lives by accepting the grace that is offered to us. Classical Catholic schools aim to do this in a conscientious way by revealing to the student who they are in God's eyes.

Anthropologie is the name of a women's clothing store, but, besides that, it is the academic term (spelled with a *y*, 'anthropology') for the study of the human person, culture, and society. When God revealed himself in Sacred Scripture, he revealed his nature as an all-knowing, just, merciful, eternal being that exists in a Trinity of persons. But this revelation through the Good News of Jesus Christ also had the converse effect of revealing to us the truth of who we are as human beings. We see ourselves most clearly when we understand ourselves through God's revelation. We understand who we are meant to be when we see ourselves reflected in the face of Christ. We see ourselves fully when we see ourselves fully loved. And we call this notion of the human person, as seen and loved by Jesus Christ, Christian anthropology. So what does this look like and how do we learn about this worldview in the classroom?

INCARNATION IN THE CLASSROOM

In chapter 1, I spoke about the importance of meta-awareness in education. The most powerful way to develop this skill in students is by examining the way we think, know, and learn. It is interesting that we spend so much time in school learning and very little time talking about what learning is and how it happens. Essentially, all learning requires us to change. The problem is that we are often very afraid to change because it means that we must be vulnerable. That is why the first goal of education is to help students feel safe and accepted for who they are. Once they know that learning is an invitation and not a requirement, they become more open to the change process.

But what change is happening in learning? One of the most powerful units that I do with my students during the four years of high school is a short unit on epistemology, the study of how we know and think. This is where you can help students to see the world in a completely new way. I start by discussing with them what it means to know something. How does the process of knowledge begin? One of my favorite lessons is when we discuss how all knowledge begins with the senses. We have to experience things to start knowing them. To make the discussion fun, I sit in the middle of the room (the tables in my classroom are arranged in a rectangle so that we are all facing each other), and I take off one of my shoes and prop my socked foot on a stool or chair. I invite a brave volunteer to come up and smell my sock. If you are wondering what this has to do with the Incarnation, bear with me. I promise this has a point.

In order to smell my foot, the student needs to come close. He or she needs to be in proximity of the thing being sensed. You cannot see things miles away, or smell things far off, or hear things in another town. It is the personal encounter that helps us to experience the world through our senses. Through this sense experience, we create imprints in our mind—not just images from seeing, but impressions from hearing, smelling, touching, and tasting as well. We know this happens because we encounter these imprints in our dreams and in our memories. One way to illustrate the point is to ask students to close their eyes. Then say a word like "chair." After opening their eyes, ask the students to describe their chair. The answers always vary. Orange, blue, brown, plastic, leather, soft, hard—the point is that I did not ask anyone to imagine anything. I just said the word. The rest we do ourselves.

Things become more profound when discussing these images in our mind. When I look at a chair, that chair is not in my mind. It stays where it is outside of me. Other people can see and experience that chair, and their impressions will be similar and different from mine. The chair that I know, however, is the image of the chair that I have produced in my mind and that is inside my head. It might be based on the one that I am experiencing, but it is a separate reality. This is when we start to talk about truth. Things are true insofar as they exist. If there is a book at your house, it does not become a book because I know it. The reality of the book is independent of me or anyone else knowing it. Think of a planet that exists in a solar system that we do not yet know. We do not know it, but that does not make it less real. This is the truth of something's existence—ontological or objective truth. When I know something, my knowledge is called true, logically true, to the degree that my impression accurately recreates the reality that is outside of me. If I see someone coming toward me and I think it is my friend, but then I discover that it is someone else, perhaps someone who looks like my friend, my initial conclusion about what my senses were telling me was incorrect. And finally, when I communicate, the degree of honesty that I use to convey the thought in my head (as long as I think that it is true—whether it is logically true or inaccurate is not the point) is called moral truth. This is the truth that is the opposite of a lie.

There is a lot of great material for discussion here and, in my experience, students are fascinated and challenged by the topic. It is always a good day in class when I have one or more students say, "Stop! You're making my brain hurt." I always take that as concrete proof that learning is taking place. People will start talking about movies like *The Matrix* and *The Truman Show* and connecting these ideas to Plato's Allegory of the Cave, or whether we can know that what I mean by "red" is the same as what you mean by "red." How can we prove it?

Many of the discussions mentioned in this section come from the fact that logic and philosophy are offered as part of our classical high school program. This lies at the heart of the discussion about how practical courses in high school ought to be: Should there be a visible correlation to job training in the courses offered or how they are offered? This is a central objective of the Common Core curriculum. "The standards were drafted by experts and teachers from across the country and are designed to ensure students are prepared for today's entry-level careers, freshman-level college courses, and workforce training programs."[2] In this paradigm, there is little justification for philosophy. Yet, I see time and time again that this class has the biggest impact on the intellectual development of children. Furthermore, there is a large focus on "critical thinking skills" in education today. Some classes might

---

2. See Fred Woeller, "What Parents Should Know about Common Core," Coeur d'Alene Press, September 8, 2014, https://cdapress.com/news/2014/sep/08/what-parents-should-know-about-common-core-5/.

have elements that develop these skills within the material, but it is the specific purpose of logic to develop critical reasoning. No class does it better. Besides these tremendous benefits, philosophy and logic also develop the metaphysical worldview that can be transformative in developing an understanding of Christian anthropology.

This awareness of how we think has many practical benefits for students as well. They learn empathy by realizing that my idea about something is the same and yet necessarily different from your idea about that thing. They can understand that liking someone will make me predisposed to find the areas of agreement in our thoughts while negative feelings toward someone will incline me to focus on the differences. They learn that knowledge is complex and that it grows rather than appears all at once. And most of all, they learn that their knowledge is only inside of them and that no one can force knowledge on them. They have to be open to knowing something and, through interactions with things and with people, to allow ideas to be born inside them. They have to allow truth to become incarnate within them. And this experience can teach them to allow the ultimate truth to become incarnate within them as well.

———❖———

Reflection from the Head of a Classical High School:
Dr. Eric DeMeuse

At the heart of nearly every student's struggle is a distorted perception of who God is. Alexis de Tocqueville writes that "there is no human action, no matter how particular we assume it to be, that does not originate in some very general human conception of God [and] of his relations with the human race." Part of the work of education is continually inviting students to reexamine the image of God they have received or created.

Every year at our high school begins with an overnight retreat. As the students and teachers pray before the Blessed Sacrament, I always present the students with two questions. I first ask them to reflect on the offenses they have committed throughout their lives—from their wrongful actions to the secret, sinful desires of the heart. I then ask them, "With all of these offenses laid bare and the punishment of a guilty verdict being death, who would you rather be judged by: an impartial judge in the US judiciary system or your father?" The students always grin a little at this question—they know that their father would in some ways be harder on them and the feeling of disappointing a loved one might devastate them, but they also know that their father wouldn't put his own child to death, making him the obvious choice as judge. I then ask the students, "Same scenario, who would you rather be judged by: an impartial judge in the US judiciary system or God?" The squirmy silence always fascinates me—the students are genuinely perplexed by this question and don't quite know how to answer. I wait a few moments and then tell them, "Students, don't you realize I asked the same question twice?"

This thought, of course, has never occurred to them. They think of God as an exacting judge "looking for someone to devour"—and they don't know their Bible well enough to realize that that descriptor belongs to the Evil One (1 Pet. 5:8). They think that their task in this life is to earn the affection of God in order to gain eternal reward. They don't yet realize that the love of God cannot be earned, but only received as an infant receives the love of a parent (see Isa. 49:15).

And so the grueling work of reforming a student's image of God begins. The students read Homer and Virgil and realize that their portrait of the Christian God oddly smacks of the vindictive deities of ancient mythologies. They read Plato and Aristotle and find the Unmoved Mover an improvement on Zeus, though ultimately too distant to be satisfying. Then they read the Old Testament and see something entirely different—a jealous God who will not let his children be prostituted despite their relentless infidelities. A God who demands the whole of us, and will stop at nothing to draw us back to himself "like a twitch upon the thread."[3] This is a God to love or hate, and at this point students face a crossroads.

I remember once meeting with a young man in my office to discuss his struggles in science class. I could tell throughout the course of the conversation that this student was struggling not with concepts or chemical equations but with the weight of proving himself—to his parents, to the world, to himself. He continued talking and grew more distressed. Finally, I looked at him and said, "I think the problem here has nothing to do with science. I think the problem here is that you don't realize how much God loves you. You need to ask God to help you realize this. Don't stop asking. Put the niceties away in prayer and be obnoxious about it. Pray to God like he's God and not some department store clerk. Ask him to show himself to you. Be bold." An elementary truth, to be sure, but one which had not yet made the eighteen-inch journey from the head to the heart.

3. This phrase, referring to God's relentless pursuit of our love, is found in the writings of G.K. Chesterton and is thematically pivotal in *Brideshead Revisited*.

Ultimately, this truth can be suggested in literature and philosophy and theology classes, but it cannot be driven home without encountering the Lord in the sacraments. A high school student needs ready access to the sacraments—to confession and the Eucharist. The words "I absolve you" not only absolve sins, and the words "This is my body" not only transform bread into Christ's flesh; they also slowly and repeatedly reform a student's image of God, and with it transform the student's self-image from a slave to a son (see Gal. 4:7).

TRUTH EXISTS, AND ITS NAME IS LOVE

Most talks or books on religion and teens start with the great difficulties experienced by many high school students today: the loneliness and the despair, the anxiety and the stress, the skyrocketing suicide rate, the dramatic increase in the use of technology. Do not get me wrong: I go on retreats with high school students where they open up and bare their souls. I know this suffering is out there. I hear it from nearly every single student as they pour out their hearts about their pains and struggles. It is real. It is intense. And it is heartbreaking to see. But this is not the book to analyze these problems.

I am not ignoring the reality or pretending it does not matter. The challenges of the modern teen are significant and specific to our modern world and modern technology. But all human beings have challenges, at every stage. Teens are not unique in having crosses to carry. Perhaps, because of puberty, they experience difficulty with a greater amount of emotional irregularity. But we all have crosses and suffering. It is the one thing we know we all share. Some crosses are bigger than others, and some of the suffering of our students is disproportionate and overwhelmingly sad. But we all need to find an answer to the question of evil and suffering in our lives. This book is about helping high school students find that answer.[4]

And the answer that Jesus has for these very difficult realities is one of the most challenging aspects of Christianity. The answer, which we have been told often but do not really internalize, is this: Embrace it. Lean into it. It is not going away. Christ is very clear about this in the Gospels. He is not here to make our hardships disappear. If you read Scripture carefully, Jesus actually promises us a greater share in his cross the closer we grow to him. But our suffering has meaning. That is the message of Christianity. It is important and valuable; in fact, it is one of the most important things that we do in life. Redemptive suffering: this is a hard truth.

Earlier, when I was speaking about amazing female heroines in ancient literature, I mentioned Iphigenia. Like so many ancient Greek stories, hers is a tragedy. But there is something beautiful in her journey. Remember the bad Greek king that I spoke about in chapter 1, Agamemnon? He is also the one who gets into a fight with the great Greek hero Achilles in the opening chapter of the *Iliad*, and he constantly reappears in the *Odyssey*, the sequel to the *Iliad*. There is a prequel to the stories of the *Iliad* and the *Odyssey*, and it is told in the story of Iphigenia.

It starts with Helen, who was the most beautiful woman in all of Greece. All of the kings in the Greek cities want to marry her. Knowing that selecting one suitor from among the many could lead to a civil war, Helen's father made all the Greek leaders promise to support whomever she chooses and to vow to fight to protect her marriage. She chooses a king named Menelaus, Agamemnon's brother. Several years later, she meets Paris, the prince of a city named Troy, falls in love with him, and escapes

4. The mental health crisis among teens is a well-known and well-documented reality, and schools have worked hard to put resources in place to help students navigate the trials and difficulties that surround them. The discussions in Socratic seminars and the experience of a fully integrated and lived faith do not in themselves remove the issue, but they do help provide teens with hope, purpose, love, and support.

with him to Troy. Although it was not the original intention of the pact among the kings of Greece, Menelaus calls on all the leaders to help him fight for Helen and bring her back. They agree and meet at the coastal city of Aulis, waiting to set sail for Troy. Thousands of men gather there.

Feeding them is no small feat, especially when the lack of wind delays their departure. Menelaus had asked his brother to oversee the army, and Agamemnon was responsible for providing the food. As provisions begin to run out, unrest overtakes the camp. Agamemnon leads a hunting party in the hills to obtain food. During the excursion, the hunters kill the sacred white stag of the temple of Artemis. For this infraction, the priest, a man named Calchas, prophesies that no wind will blow until the sin has been wiped away. In order to obtain forgiveness for the transgression of killing the sacred deer, Calchas proclaims that the goddess demands that Agamemnon sacrifice his daughter Iphigenia.

The rest of the story is heart wrenching and oddly beautiful. Agamemnon, mind-bogglingly, agrees to the sacrifice, but, for obvious reasons, does not want his wife and daughter to know. (If you have not guessed, I am not a big fan of Agamemnon. Neither was his wife, Clytemnestra, the one who later killed him for what he did to their daughter.) Agamemnon decides to trick his daughter to come to the camp by telling her that she is to marry the great Greek hero Achilles. Now the fight at the beginning of the *Iliad* and the rage of Achilles start to make sense.

Agamemnon pathetically writes to his wife that there is no need for her to bother with the journey. Obviously, she completely ignores him. Excited for her beautiful, pure, and innocent daughter, they set out together for Aulis. When they get close to the camp, they run into Achilles. Things unravel quickly when they discover that Achilles has no idea about the fictitious marriage proposal, and Agamemnon's deceit is soon discovered. He doubles down, however, and says he must go through with the demands of the goddess. The twist is that Achilles is touched by the goodness and bravery of Iphigenia and offers to marry her and defend her from her father. Iphigenia, who implores her father to change his mind at first, eventually decides that she must make this sacrifice for Greece, the same sacrifice that all the soldiers are willing to make.

Despite all of the severe dysfunction in this ancient story, it points to a simple truth that reverberates through all of literature and history in nearly every culture at nearly every time: When a guilty person suffers for the wrong that they do, we call it a punishment. But when someone innocent dies because of the sins of others, we call it a sacrifice. And their sacrifice brings atonement for the sins of others. This is the major theme of the *Iliad*, in which Hector's death brings an end to Achilles' anger. This theme is constant in Shakespeare: the deaths of Romeo and Juliet restore peace between their two families; Ophelia dies to restore goodness to the court of Denmark. (Nearly everyone else in *Hamlet* dies, but their death is punishment, not sacrifice.) But it is not just in the stories of the ancient world and the Renaissance. Uncle Ben's (or Aunt May's) death leads to Peter Parker becoming a hero and not a villain. Black Widow and Iron Man die to reverse the damage done by Thanos. Besides literature and movies, we see this truth play out in history as well with the deaths of the martyrs and heroic men and women willing to sacrifice their lives for a just cause. And, ultimately, this is the meaning of the suffering and death of Jesus Christ. He is the most pure and innocent person to ever live, and his sacrifice is greater than any made by anyone else, ever. It frees us from our sins.

Somehow we know this truth intuitively: that sacrifice is good and noble, that suffering for others is one of the most beautiful and purifying ideals we can imagine. We see it in the pagan world and in the literature of other cultures before the message of Christianity reached them. It is an instinctive truth. And it is in the light of this truth that we can uncover a deeper meaning to our own suffering and pain. Suffering is a very real and significant component of the lives of high schoolers, and it is painful. If it is not, it is not suffering. It is raw, and it is often unfair. It is intense, and we feel lost when we are in it. Hope does not deny suffering; it does not tell us to pull ourselves up by our bootstraps or give simple, sometimes offensive, explanations for our pain. Hope calls us to trust: to trust in a love and a truth that is greater than us and our pain, to suffer with and for others. The suffering is unavoidable; the meaning is found in love.

CHRISTIAN ANTHROPOLOGY

All education is incarnational by nature. The learning process gives life to new ideas in the student. Truth is born again for the first time. This is why education is a journey for truth, but it is also a journey for love. Providing a space in high school for students to encounter the love of God means more than being a school with occasional Mass and religion class. Everything about the school needs to point to the reality of God's love. Classical Catholic education is at its best when all aspects of community and academic life point to this one reality. Christ needs to be present in the activities, the clubs, and the sports along with the liturgical life. And Christ needs to be fully incarnate in the classroom—not just theology but every class. He needs to be revealed in the books that are chosen and the way they are taught. His love needs to be present in the pedagogy and the discipline of the school. Everything needs to point to Christ. This allows the school to saturate the students in the Catholic view of the human person. It allows these young men and women to understand themselves through the love of Christ, the embrace of the Father, and the indwelling of the Holy Spirit. When schools can create this environment, students will encounter God's love and grow in his grace. This is what classical Catholic education does so well. Through an integrated curriculum focused on the Incarnation, seminar discussion centered on student discovery, exposure to ideas that are archetypal and profound with an emphasis on a metaphysical worldview, the current revival of classical Catholic education is able to achieve something that alludes many non-classical Catholic schools.

One of the greatest obstacles, as I mentioned earlier, is the deep-rooted doubt in students that they are worthy of unconditional love. Perhaps it has to do with the hormones of puberty, but students in ninth and tenth grade especially seem to have an interior conviction that, at their core, they are unlovable. Add to this the stress, anxiety, loneliness, and pain of the average high school student, and you have an existential need for God's loving embrace that gives meaning and provides healing for their pain and isolation. And this fact is important for creating our educational spaces. The most important thing our students need to learn is that they are loved. When this takes place, all learning happens easier, faster, and more naturally. Students who are whole and who feel safe and accepted learn better. Students who struggle with doubt and insecurity and pain have more obstacles in the process of education and knowledge assimilation. When they are loved, they will learn.

My all-time favorite character in literature is the Bishop of Digne. He is the best example of the mercy that all people, especially high school students, crave with their whole being. His goodness is the very essence of purifying suffering. In a certain way, we can feel the mercy of God on us as we see this humble man of God give mercy to the most rejected, the most hardened, the most castaway member of society. He appears at the beginning of my all-time favorite book, *Les Misérables* by Victor Hugo. It is a big book, and the author is in no hurry to finish telling his story. That is why the first section, fourteen chapters long, is dedicated to the background of this fictitious but amazing priest. The Bishop of Digne is most well known for his interaction with the paroled convict Jean Valjean. After serving nineteen years in prison for no real reason, Valjean is released. As an ex-convict, however, there is nowhere he can go and nothing he can do to begin to rebuild his life, until the night he knocks violently at the bishop's door.

Word of this dangerous traveler had spread through the village, but the bishop invites the convict in and sits with him at table. Dining together, Valjean is overcome by, yet at the same time incredulous of, the humanity of the bishop. He does not trust anyone to treat him with dignity. The bishop offers him a bed for the night, and when Valjean prods that he might be an assassin, the good priest offers no judgment but entrusts them both to God's protection.

The bishop's words seem naïve when Valjean awakens later that night and stands in the bishop's room contemplating whether he should murder his host. Seeing a crucifix on the wall above the priest's bed with an arm outstretched in love to the bishop and another with forgiveness for him, Valjean instead decides to steal all the silver he can find and flee in the night. The next morning, the police arrive at the bishop's residence with the escaped thief, ready to return him to jail for the remainder of his days. The police, called by the French name *gendarmes*, present the criminal and mockingly relate the man's claim that the bishop had gifted him with the bag of silver that he is carrying. The following short interaction is probably one of the most beautiful passages in all of literature.

"Ah! here you are!" [the bishop] exclaimed, looking at Jean Valjean. "I am glad to see you. Well, but how is this? I gave you the candlesticks too, which are of silver like the rest, and for which you can certainly get two hundred francs. Why did you not carry them away with your forks and spoons?" . . .

"Do not forget, never forget, that you have promised to use this money in becoming an honest man."

Jean Valjean, who had no recollection of ever having promised anything, remained speechless. The Bishop had emphasized the words when he uttered them. He resumed with solemnity:—

"Jean Valjean, my brother, you no longer belong to evil, but to good. It is your soul that I buy from you; I withdraw it from black thoughts and the spirit of perdition, and I give it to God."[5]

This is the love we crave. This is the love that is promised to us. This is the love that became human in the Incarnation.

WITH TRUTH COMES FREEDOM

Exploring the truth in a way that respects the needs of the individual is essential to classical education. What pedagogical methods aspire to achieve through differentiated learning, classical education incorporates at an essential level. Acknowledging the needs of each individual in the educational process, differentiated learning speaks to the skill of adjusting the level of learning or the pace of knowledge acquisition to meet these varying needs. Teachers study, train, and work very hard to build this process into their classrooms, and it is of great benefit to their students. Classical education also highly values the need for differentiated learning. However, for the classical classroom, education is naturally tailored to the needs of the individual through the pedagogical methodology.

This has already been demonstrated through the application of the Socratic Method in the classroom. But seminar discussions are just one way in which classical pedagogy tailors the educational process to the individual. Beyond integrated, discussion-based learning, the core of classical instruction is based on student discovery and individual pacing. This can be seen in the art of

5. Victor Hugo, *Les Misérables*, trans. Isabel Hapgood, Full Text Archive, https://www.fulltextarchive.com/book/les-miserables-by-victor-hugo-trans-isabel-f/3/.

communication that provides an arc to the language arts curriculum from the early years of school through high school.

The art of communication, known as rhetoric, comprises several composite skills that accompany a student throughout their school career. In the classical high school, rhetoric builds on elementary skills of narration, memorization, recitation, writing, and reading, which are fundamental core skills that classical education prioritizes. With this firm foundation, rhetoric seeks to help students give verbal expression and color to the truth that has been born within them. As students learn to give expression to this interior truth, either orally in discussions and presentations or verbally in essays and written projects, the art of communication becomes central in their learning journey.

Rhetoric is considered one of the seven liberal arts. In today's world, the liberal arts can be interpreted as the skills needed to develop critical, independent thinking skills in order to be free from societal groupthink or pressure. When examined, the skill of rhetoric has traditionally been understood to incorporate three essential elements: logos, pathos, and ethos. Logos refers to the truth of a thing as objective reality and the logical argument with which it gets presented. But the art of communication demands more than just skill in presentation. The rhetorician is also one who can empathize with the emotions of an audience, be it one or many. This is the skill of pathos. Finally, the organic unity in the classical mindset is demonstrated by the addition of a third requirement of the student of rhetoric, ethos. This refers to the need for the speaker to be authentic, virtuous, honest, and transparent in their communication, but even, more importantly, in their lives. In developing these skills, each student must confront their ignorance, grow in knowledge, understand the needs of those with whom they are speaking, and live in a manner that is virtuous and inspiring. Beyond educational differentiation, this demonstrates the desire of classical education to meet the needs of each individual student as they aspire to personal excellence, virtue, and holiness.

SUMMARY

The birth of Christ changed the human story and provided an answer to our longing and desire. What Hector symbolized, Jesus incarnated. And this Incarnation of the Son of God as man changes how the human person understands who they are, where they are, and why they are. It helps us to understand the depths of the love that is offered to us as sons and daughters of God. Through the reality of this love, we learn to see ourselves differently, with a more profound dignity and worth, and a greater calling and purpose. The evil of suffering that plagues us all takes on a purpose and a meaning that make it part of our spiritual relationship rather than a hindrance. This is the full impact of the Catholic worldview, the Christian anthropology.

The Incarnation provides a deeper understanding of God's design in creation and creates the Christian worldview. The logical harmony and internal beauty to which Christ bore witness is seen in the human person, in the study of our biology, and in the epistemological process by which we learn. All learning is essentially incarnational, giving birth in us to a truth that exists independently outside of us. But the revelation of the person of Christ also helps us to understand the most difficult aspect of our life: evil and suffering. The beautiful but challenging story of the Greek heroine Iphigenia shows that the truth of sacrificial love that we see in Christ's redemptive death on the cross is an innate truth that is continually present in the literature of every century. Ultimately, our deepest desire is to experience the mercy and unconditional love of the Father. This is the desire of all humanity, but perhaps no one experiences this need more acutely than those in high school. The Bishop of Digne, who appears on the first pages of *Les Misérables*, illustrates divine mercy in a way so profound that it parallels the beauty of Christ's parable of the prodigal son. Finally, by developing the art of communication, or rhetoric, the classical school helps students to give expression to the truth that was born inside of them with compassion and authenticity.

6

Christendom

Scholars and Saints

TWO REBELLIOUS TEENAGERS

We are all called to holiness at every stage of life. But it does seem that, in history, it is often the young that embrace the call to holiness. This might seem counterintuitive, but I have noticed how hard it is for people of middle age to take on the rigor of spiritual growth. Not that it cannot be done, but I think it is harder. Young people have great zeal. Though this can also lead to rebelliousness, for some, this very rebelliousness is integral to their path of sanctity.

St. Thomas Aquinas and St. Francis of Assisi are two of the most well-known and respected saints of the Catholic Church. Each, in their own way, was a revolutionary. The story of St. Francis is particularly popular. After his conversion to Christ, his *kairos*, he embraced the Gospel demands of poverty, simplicity, and charity with incredible zeal and enthusiasm. The story involving his father is especially poignant and highlights some of the differences between the developing brain (Francis was in his early twenties at the time of this story) and the practicality of parents. Having sold merchandise from his father's business without permission in order to fund one of his church projects, Francis found himself in the public square of Assisi, in front of the local bishop, publicly accused of theft by his father, Don Pietro. Francis famously stripped himself of all of his clothes, returned them to his father, renounced his inheritance, and walked off into the imagination of those aspiring to live a holy life. As is common with St. Francis, the story is somewhat romanticized. The truth was far more complicated and raw, involving Francis being beaten and even imprisoned by his father prior to the famous confrontation.

These extreme parenting techniques were experienced by St. Thomas Aquinas as well in a similarly well-known historical anecdote.[1] About forty years after the confrontation in the town square of Assisi, Thomas, at the age of sixteen, was kidnapped by his brothers as he traveled to Rome and locked in a cell within the family castle in Aquino in southern Italy. His family was upset because they had wanted him to be abbot of the nearby Benedictine monastery Monte Cassino. This would have been a position of influence and prestige. Instead, the rebellious youth wanted to join one of the new "begging" religious groups, the Dominicans. As with Don Pietro, Thomas' father saw this zealous religious impulse as naïve, embarrassing, and unacceptable. In order to temper Thomas' saintly aspirations, the story goes that the family even employed a prostitute to seduce the now seventeen-year-old boy, who was still held in the castle prison, into succumbing to the desires of the flesh. Surely this would cure him of his religious fervor. But Thomas chased her out of his cell with a torch and slammed the door.

THE REAL AGE OF ENLIGHTENMENT

Deeply rooted within the human psyche is a longing for redemption and a reunification that will make us whole. In the ancient world, even without a Jewish or Christian vocabulary to express these ideas, we can see these desires written in the works of the great philosophers, mathematicians, poets, and scientists. Much has been written about this human longing throughout the centuries.

1. G.K. Chesterton's work on St. Thomas has thought-provoking insights on this particular event in the life of the saint. See "The Runaway Abbot" in his book *St. Thomas Aquinas*.

The greatest works of literature, even those with sweeping, epic backdrops, usually focus on one character's journey to find peace, to find home, to find (divine) love. This is the case with the *Iliad* and the *Odyssey*; it is the main theme of St. Augustine's *Confessions*; and it is the main drama in *Les Misérables, Crime and Punishment,* and *War and Peace.* The longing within humanity for personal redemption is on display throughout history.

The modern world has rejected this desire, however, as well as the Author of all our desiring. This rejection of God has increased within the intellectual tradition and in society over the past four hundred years. Today, belief in God seems outdated to many. But this has not extinguished their longing for "something more." And as humanity in the Western world grows further and further from God, our understanding of ourselves and our ability to find happiness has decreased rather than grown. The reality of this secular anthropology and its impact on education and the modern high school experience will be the subject of the next chapter.

But in between the longing and fulfillment on the one hand and the modern rejection on the other is the oft-overlooked period of the High Middle Ages. Often dismissed as backward or irrelevant, this age, the time of Christendom, produced many of the best aspects of our modern world. This period gave rise to universities and hospitals, some of the greatest architecture and art in the world, and some of the greatest saints and scholars of history: St. Catherine of Siena, St. Thomas and St. Francis, St. Joan of Arc, and others. This was the age of faith and reason, of profound human achievement and advancement, of growth in holiness. Despite the claims of the eighteenth century, this was the true Age of Enlightenment.

THE RISE OF SCHOOLS

After the death of Plato, his star student, Aristotle, assumed he would be named head of the Academy. When this did not happen, Aristotle decided to leave Athens and take a position as tutor to the son of King Philip II of Macedon. The student was Alexander, who would eventually become known as Alexander the Great for conquering most of the known world. While Alexander was busy waging his military campaigns, Aristotle returned to Athens and started a rival school, the Lyceum. But a shift had begun to take place. Over the course of the next hundred years, the center of learning would move from Greece to Egypt, to the city named after Aristotle's student: Alexandria.

The greatest library of the ancient world was in Alexandria, Egypt. With the largest collection of manuscripts, it held the key to vast knowledge and required those of learning, or desirous of learning, to travel as pilgrims to its doors. No description of the building is known to us. Everyone seemed to only care about what the library contained and not the building itself. Despite the tens of thousands of scrolls, including the works of Plato and Aristotle, the library gradually fell into disrepair over the centuries before the Roman Empire began to crumble. Julius Caesar, in his exploits in Egypt with Cleopatra, accidentally burned a part of the library as he attempted to destroy the naval forces of a foe.

After the fall of the Roman Empire, the centers of learning switched to the monasteries. These houses of prayer provided oases of security and stability and became safe havens of the intellectual tradition in times of tumult and war throughout the first centuries of Christian history. Because of the importance of reading Scripture, prayer books, and theological texts, cathedrals and monasteries developed their own schools to teach young monks to read and write. This led naturally to their work as scribes but also to the growth of learning in theology, philosophy, education, medicine, government, etc.

Around the dawn of the second millennium, from these religious origins, institutions of higher learning began to grow. A medical university in Salerno, Italy, was established in the ninth century as the first Western university, attracting students from across Europe. Two hundred years later, a respected school of law was founded in Bologna. Shortly thereafter, universities began to arise in Paris, Oxford, and many of the major cities of Europe. Nearly all of these universities had a core set of classes that were based on the seven liberal arts. These were the disciplines that were needed to be an active, free member of society and were divided into the trivium, which focused on language acquisition, and the quadrivium, which studied space and time. The trivium consisted of the study of grammar, logic, and rhetoric. Within the four subjects of the quadrivium, geometry and astronomy were related to space, while math and music were related to harmony and time. 'Core curriculum' and 'liberal arts college' are terms still used today in most institutions of higher learning, although the original meaning and importance are nearly completely lost.

METAPHYSICS AND MYSTICS . . . AND REBELS

The works of Aristotle were highly regarded during antiquity and the first centuries of Christianity. The library of Alexandria boasted a complete set of the great sage's works. This influence began to wane, however, toward the end of the Roman Empire. Neoplatonism, a form of philosophy that synthesized the teaching of Plato with elements of spirituality, had a significant influence on Christianity of late antiquity. St. Augustine, for example, attributed the completion of the intellectual part of his conversion to Neoplatonism. At the same time, distrust of Aristotle began to grow. St. Jerome complained that heretics had a penchant for quoting Plato's student.

After Islam had established itself in the world, the works of Aristotle began to have influence in the Arab arena, particularly his treatises on logic and metaphysics. Eventually, this intellectual tradition resulted in one of the most influential Islamic philosophers, Ibn Sina, better known in the West as Avicenna, incorporating the works of Aristotle and other great Greek thinkers with Islamic thinking. With over 240 titles to his name, this great philosopher had the same encyclopedic expanse in the fields of philosophy, science, and medicine as Aristotle before him and Thomas after him. A brilliant and polemical figure, not unlike Socrates, Avicenna incorporated the thought of ancient Greece, liberally and unapologetically, into his Muslim worldview. This paved the way for another great Muslim philosopher, Ibn Rushd, also known as Averroes, to translate and comment on the entire corpus of Aristotle's work in the twelfth century. "We must accept from our predecessors, whether they share our religion or not, whatever accords with the truth," he states in his work *On the Harmony of Religion and Philosophy*.[2]

Through the influence of these Arab thinkers, one of the greatest thinkers of the Catholic Church, St. Thomas Aquinas, was exposed to the teaching of Aristotle. By reconciling this philosophical system with the deposit of faith, Thomas was able to enrich the Church's theological understanding of the spiritual and created order. Like the great thinkers before him, he was a rebel and a revolutionary, with an openness to truth regardless of the consequences. As such, Thomas provides the perfect model for the synthesis of classical and Catholic education, for he was not only a metaphysician but a mystic. He was a man of philosophy and someone with an intense, intimate relationship with God. And both the metaphysician and the mystic see the unity of reality in the world around them. Underneath the experiences of the senses, they discover a universal and all-embracing harmony. Three years after his death, in a great irony of history, several of Aquinas' teachings were condemned as heresy by a local bishop. But Thomas was canonized a saint less than fifty years later. His work, and the influence of Aristotle, had not only been rehabilitated but would gain a privileged place in Catholic theology. The Church had formally embraced a metaphysical mysticism and a

2. Sebastian Günther, "Ibn Rushd and Thomas Aquinas on Education," in *The Heritage of Arabo-Islamic Learning: Studies Presented to Wadad Kadi*, ed. Maurice A. Pomerantz and Aram A. Shahin (Leiden: Brill, 2016), 250.

holy metaphysics.[3] This was the revolution of St. Thomas. But being a rebel is not something unique to the journey of the saints. Teenagers are often known to have a rebellious streak as well. And perhaps this tendency speaks to their desire for something more, something extraordinary, something that answers their greatest questions and longings. If so, then challenging high school students to strive for great holiness in their lives will direct them to the ultimate answer that they are seeking in their rebellion.

Personal Reflections from Two Rebellious Teenagers: Haley and Abby

Haley: It was the first day of spring break during my freshman year of high school, and the last thing I wanted to do was wake up early. But that Thursday, I found myself rolling out of bed while it was still dark outside, dragging my friend Abby with me. The two of us joined my younger sister and my mom in our minivan and took off, abuzz with nerves about what we would encounter once the car was parked.

We had prayed at abortion facilities before, but this was our first time praying at the Planned Parenthood downtown. My sister, Abby, and I timidly huddled beside the clinic's brick wall while my mom began reciting the Rosary. Softly, we mumbled along with her: "Hail Mary, full of grace . . ." Suddenly, a middle-aged man charged at us, yelling that we ought to be ashamed of ourselves because we were "racists" who should "go pray at home." My mom attempted to calm him down, but he was undeterred. After a few more insults, he walked away and we breathed a sigh of relief,

---

3. For a discussion on the relationship of metaphysics and mysticism, see Heather M. Erb, "Being and the Mystic: The Metaphysical Foundations of Thomas Aquinas' Mystical Thought," *Verbum* 6, no. 1 (April 2004), https://verbum.ppke.hu/index.php/verbum /article/view/200/170.

assuming that was the end of our interaction with the angry stranger.

When our prayer hour ended, we prepared to leave. As we started walking we saw the man who had confronted us crossing the street, this time recording us with his phone. My mom quickly stepped between him and us, but when it became clear that he wouldn't be reasoned with, she ushered us away. He shouted after us as we went, calling us "white pseudo-Christians." My sister and I laughed when Abby, who is clearly of Mexican descent, retorted that she was "pretty far from white."

Abby: "You girls will end up here one day." These words were used once upon a time to wound my sense of truth, a low blow to shut me up and silence my faith. When trying to describe my journey of faith, I did not realize it would be one standout event that would solidify so much—not until of course that one event happened.

One sunny April day in 2019, I stood adjacent to a Planned Parenthood doing nothing more than silently praying for the women and the children facing life-altering, life-ending circumstances. About an hour into this endeavor, Pennsylvania Representative Brian Sims, irate to say the least, came bounding at my best friend Haley and me. He was filming us, shouting at us, threatening us. In utter transparency, I have forgotten much of the language he threw at us, but eight words have stuck relentlessly with me: "You girls will end up here one day." I assume he was referring to us having to utilize Planned Parenthood's abortion services in our futures. He said this to two freshmen in high school. Two fourteen-year-old girls. He said it to stun us. To shame and minimize us.

Haley: Easter passed, and we soon forgot about the incident. But two weeks later, things took a dramatic turn. While at dinner, my father's phone started buzzing. Friends were calling to tell us that the man who accosted us had posted the video online and that Live Action had found his post and was publicly condemning his behavior. It was then that we discovered that our harasser had identified himself in his own video as State Representative Brian Sims, before offering $100 in exchange for our identities. Millions of people viewed the video and saw this for what it was: an elected official trying to intimidate three teenagers out of exercising their constitutional right to peacefully protest. The fact of a middle-aged man doxing underage high school girls made the story especially disturbing.

The following days were chaotic. We welcomed support from friends by day, while a police car was stationed outside our house by night. Five days after the video exploded, fifteen hundred people attended a rally headlined by Lila Rose, Abby Johnson, and Matt Walsh in the exact spot where we had been accosted. Our family decided to use the attention for good and organized a GoFundMe for the Pro-Life Union of Greater Philadelphia that raised over $125,000.

While there was a great amount of good that came out of this experience, Abby and I were unsure of how our lives would look once the word got out to our school community. We both attended a diocesan Catholic high school in Pennsylvania. Over the next week, we debated whether we should even tell our friends, unsure of how people would react. I vividly remember a FaceTime conversation that took place the night before Easter break ended, during which we both decided not to bring up the incident. Freshman year was hard enough without being labeled "crazy pro-lifers."

Abby and I tentatively walked to our lockers on Tuesday and were ambushed by a rush of our peers. We braced ourselves, but to our surprise, the words surrounding us were those of encouragement and kindness. That first day back in school, we were stunned by the amount of people who came up to offer their support. Upperclassmen we had been too scared to speak to stopped us in the hallway, commenting on how crazy our experience was and how we looked "so chill" on the video. The love only continued as the weeks went on, and my mom was on the news a few times to speak about the incident. Teachers, students, and administrators all pulled us aside in school to see how we were doing. This experience with Rep. Sims taught us that hatred and intolerance do exist. But most importantly, this experience has taught us about ourselves, our faith, and our inner strength. It has shown us what is important, the importance of a supportive environment, and who we will be as we continue through high school and college.

Abby: Had the gross, pugnacious demeanor of Rep. Sims worked in the way he intended it to, I would have run from my freedom of speech and the freedom to stand for what I believe is right. Mr. Sims would be disappointed to discover that instead it has fueled my drive for justice and my desire to live an authentic and deep Christian life. Had it not been for this interaction, I might not have become president of my school's Respect Life Club. His threats did not silence me but gave me a voice. And through his abusive actions, I have learned to trust in the grace of God, to live out my Catholic faith, and to search for his will for my life.

DATING IN HIGH SCHOOL

Having a strong, healthy relationship with Christ is important. But it is just the beginning. The life of love to which the Lord calls us is anything but basic. In fact, the reality of the overwhelming love that God offers us—not just in heaven but in this life as well—is staggering. This is the full implication of the reality of God entering and transforming humanity. This presence not only changed history, the culture, and the world: it changed us and the possibility of who we can become.

Very often in classical Catholic high schools, there is talk about "the next generation of saints" or "making saints," but these ideals need concrete spiritual theology so that they do not become hollow slogans. Those words encapsulate God's covenantal design of intense spiritual union with us but often do not get explained with the full weight of what is being promised by Scripture and the Church. Saints are those who have opened themselves fully to God's grace and have been radically transformed by the divine life within. Holiness is more than a basic adherence to the minimum directives of the Church. The explicit details of what is promised in the spiritual life and how to attain this goal are vitally important for high school students, and anyone else, to learn. And it is revolutionary.

Another great saint and rebel of this period, Bernard of Clairvaux, once said (and I am paraphrasing) that even though many people practice the faith, very few strive for a relationship of deep intimacy with the Triune God who dwells within us through grace. Pope St. John Paul II once said to a group of bishops that "your first duty as pastors is not projects and organizations, but to lead people to a deep intimacy with the Trinity."[4] I think what the Holy Father said to the bishops applies equally to Catholic school administrators and teachers.

The word 'patrimony' refers to the inheritance that children are entitled to from their father. This deep experience of God's love is our patrimony. Scripture, the Church, and the saints are very clear about this. Many saints have spoken about the spiritual life and how this spiritual relationship unfolds. Some of them are considered experts. And the Church has specifically pointed to a few canonized authors and titled them Doctors of the Church. Two of these great saints are St. Teresa of Avila and St. John of the Cross, both from sixteenth-century Spain and both revolutionaries in their own right. They each give detailed accounts and

4. Thomas Dubay, *Deep Conversion / Deep Prayer* (San Francisco: Ignatius, 2006), 5.

descriptions of the various stages of growth in our relationship with Jesus Christ.

In his many writings, St. John of the Cross compares our spiritual journey to that of a bride searching for her groom or to climbing a mountain. This last metaphor is explored at length in his famous work *Ascent of Mount Carmel*. Here, St. John teaches about the importance of asceticism and purification in the spiritual life. If teachers are to help students to encounter the love of Christ through their classroom and the religious practices of the school, then they take on a special role as spiritual guides for their students. This means that we must form our teachers in the basic tenets of spiritual growth so that they can be a model and resource for the students in the spiritual life.

Along with St. John of the Cross, his contemporary St. Teresa of Avila is put forward by the Church as a trustworthy authority on the spiritual journey. St. Teresa has a famous metaphor of seven mansions or dwellings, each built within the next so that they are like concentric circles leading one into the seventh dwelling in the center. The first three mansions are ascetical, meaning that we have to do some work to purify ourselves by getting rid of bad habits and replacing them with good ones. We enter the first mansion by acknowledging our sinfulness, accepting and trusting God's forgiveness, incorporating prayer into our daily schedule, avoiding sin, and avoiding people, places, and things that might lead us into sin. Much of our school culture promotes the life of the first mansion. Someone could spend their whole spiritual life at this level. But for those who accept the grace to persist in doing good and building an intimate prayer life, they enter the second mansion. The second mansion is all about learning to rely on God when things are tough and dedicating yourself to growing closer to him. There will be trials at this stage of the spiritual life—people and things that might tempt you to fall back into your old life. It is not easy, but with the help of good family and friends, perhaps a spiritual director, and the sacraments, your newfound trust in

God will carry you through. In prayer, we start to get a hint of an awareness of God's presence within us. The third mansion is populated by people who lead beautiful lives of virtue and service to God. To keep with Teresa's metaphor, these people have moved far away from the life outside the castle walls. By accepting God's grace and allowing it to flow through their lives, they have come to a place of holiness and beauty, bringing peace, joy, and kindness to their surroundings.

When I said that we can have a personal encounter with Christ in earlier chapters, not only was I not exaggerating—I was completely underselling what our relationship with God can be. As we enter into the last four mansions of St. Teresa's interior castle, our world changes completely. In the fourth mansion, we start to have a sense of God's presence. It is usually experienced as a profound sense of peace that gently washes over our soul. It can last for minutes, hours, or days. This type of prayer then intensifies to an awareness of God's actual presence within us. We experience him loving us. This is not an exaggeration or figurative language; it is a beautiful reality. Read a summary of St. Teresa's seven mansions. I once spent a few years in a monastery surrounded by some very holy people, people who spent their days in this loving awareness of God. I have known people who are married and who live regular lives who have experienced this. I have seen and helped people grow into the fourth mansion and beyond. I have experienced it myself at one point in my life. God is present within, and once we awaken to the reality of God's presence in us, our lives will never be the same. The sixth and seventh mansions are our spiritual betrothal and marriage to the Bridegroom. As we saw earlier, Scripture explains the meaning of our covenantal marriage with God. In fact, all of Scripture can be explained as one journey to get us back to the Garden and under the tree so that we can be married to the Lamb who was slain, as described in the last chapters of the Bible. This is the full meaning of the mystery of the Eucharist and of Marriage. "This is my body." This is paradise, the eternal wedding feast of the Lamb.

When I tell my students about the possibilities of what our relationship with God could and should look like and give them a concrete plan of how to get there, they are overwhelmed and excited. At first they just stare at me with wide eyes and open mouths. They wonder why no one has ever told them this before. But this is how we are meant to live. When God created us, he made us his children. When we turned from him and sinned, he made up for our fault so that we could be restored to him as sons and daughters. He is constantly inviting us and waiting for us. Forgiving us and calling to us. God did not come simply to be our friend. He came to bring us into profound divine intimacy. It is a revolutionary type of love and a call that makes us rebels for the ultimate cause. This is why St. Francis stripped naked in the town square and why St. Thomas was able to embrace chastity in an extremely tempting situation. Teenagers are ready and are looking for this love, and it is the foremost love that they will find in life. We must help them find it. This is the most important dating that students can do in high school.

SUMMARY

Saints are rebels. Answering the call of God's intense desire for a relationship produces a revolution within our lives and the world around us. This was certainly the case with two of the great saints of Christendom, St. Francis of Assisi and St. Thomas Aquinas. Both of these great examples of Christian holiness dedicated themselves to God at a young age and are wonderful examples of the holy zeal to which teenagers can aspire.

The revelation of God's love in Jesus Christ transformed the world. The growing impact of the Incarnation on civilization resulted in a society that celebrated the harmony between faith and reason. The history of education and the birth of the university cannot be understood apart from Christendom. After the fall of the

Roman Empire, it was the monasteries that kept learning alive in the West. Eventually, this led to the formation of great centers of learning—universities—throughout Europe. In the Arab world, learning and study were also flourishing. A special importance was given to the works of Aristotle, which, although they had lost prominence in the West, continued to influence the works of great Islamic philosophers. Through this influence, the works of Aristotle came into the hands of Thomas Aquinas, who started a revolution of deeper understanding in Catholic theology by integrating the insights of this great philosopher with the deposit of faith. So influential was this thinker on Aquinas that the latter would refer to Aristotle simply as "the Philosopher."

But the revolution of this period also extended to our understanding of spiritual life. Two of the greatest writers and guides on growing in intimacy with God, St. Teresa of Avila and St. John of the Cross, started a renewal of their religious order, the Carmelites, and left the Church a trustworthy description of how to open oneself to this divine intimacy. God's love is revolutionary, and this is the love that teenagers need to hear about. This is the love that fulfills our greatest longings. This is the love that should be taught in high school.

The Modern Era

Secular Anthropology

THE PARDONER'S TALE

Thomas Becket, Archbishop of Canterbury, was famously assassinated in December 1170 as a result of a conflict that had arisen between him and King Henry II of England. His burial shrine soon became a site of pilgrimage, and it is to the relics of this great martyr saint that a group of thirty pilgrims set out from London some two hundred years later. To keep themselves occupied during the journey, they agreed to a storytelling competition. One of the pilgrims was a pardoner by trade, which meant that he sold relics, the bones or clothing of saints, as a source of livelihood. His entry into the competition has become one of the more famous stories told in Chaucer's *Canterbury Tales*. The moral of his story is that greed is the root of all evil.

In the tale, three men learn of the death of a friend. Angered, they wish to avenge themselves upon Death and set out to track it down. An old man they encounter on the road informs them that he has seen Death under a tree in a nearby garden. The three companions rush to the spot only to find a large pile of gold instead. One of them is sent back to town to retrieve a bag to carry the precious cargo. When he returns, the two companions jump upon him and kill him. To celebrate their good fortune they sit down and enjoy the wine their dead friend brought back with him. Soon all three lie dead under the tree, the last two from the poison that their companion had placed in the wine. *Greed is the root of all evil.*

The tale might sound vaguely familiar, as J.K. Rowling found inspiration in the story for the tale of the Deathly Hallows in the last installment of the Harry Potter series.[1] What is of greater interest than the story, however, is the insight that the Pardoner gives about the state of Christendom in the later Middle Ages. Before he begins his tale, the Pardoner shares openly that he is corrupt, knowingly selling false relics to gullible believers. He makes no apology for his simony. Instead, he boasts of his greed and gluttony while making a living preaching to others to avoid these exact sins. That he proclaims his sacrilege so openly and unapologetically, in the middle of a pilgrimage, shows that all was not well in Christendom. The zeal and spiritual love of St. Thomas Becket and St. Francis had begun to dissipate. The harmony of faith and reason had become strained. In Christendom, where there is no personal relationship with Christ to ground the faith, sin can grow freely.

THE SEEDS OF DOUBT

There are many virtues, and all of them are worth cultivating. Patience, prudence, magnanimity, courage, and the like are always good patterns of behavior that are important to develop in every circumstance. Aristotle calls this character excellence. There are three virtues, however, that pertain directly to our relationship with God and are therefore called the theological virtues: faith, hope, and charity. We have faith in God, hope in God, and love for God. Of all the virtues, these three speak to our relationship with the divine, whereas other virtues help us do the right thing

---

1. See the article by Lindsay Toler, "Chaucer Inspired Deathly Hallows: Rowling," The Age, August 3, 2007, https://www.theage.com.au/entertainment/books/chaucer -inspired-deathly-hallows-rowling-20070803-ge5hu5.html, for a discussion about the Pardoner's Tale as the inspiration for the tale of the Deathly Hallows within the final book of the Harry Potter series.

in our relationship with others. But these virtues are more intricate than we might at first realize.

The word 'faith' refers to three related but different things—so different in fact that we can almost speak of the word 'faith' as a homonym. The fact that we use the three meanings interchangeably without distinguishing between them causes a great deal of confusion when people speak about the teachings of the Church. The first usage references a body of truths. "Confession of faith," "This is the faith," etc., are statements that refer to an objective deposit of revealed knowledge, often expressed in a creed. In a second usage, the term 'faith' is a personal decision, an agreement on our part with the objective reality of what the Church teaches. We have faith in the faith. This personal assent is an act of the individual, but requires the grace of faith from God in order to fully embrace God's revelation with our whole being. This grace, a third aspect of faith, is a free gift from God that we can either accept or reject. We can grow in our faith insofar as it is a personal act, but the gift of faith from God can only be received. Faith allows us to have faith in the faith.[2]

The greatest theological virtue is love. But, again, this concept is complex and admits of several distinct layers. As seen in chapter 4, the Greeks were far more nuanced in their vocabulary on this subject. They had multiple words to describe the various forms of love between individuals. The word *eros* refers to sexual love, from which we get the word 'erotic.' The love found in friendship is called *philia*, and this in turn has several layers: friendship of utility, friendship of pleasure, and friendship of virtue. *Agape* love is the self-sacrificial love that we see in God, and perhaps in a parent. There are other forms of love that the Greeks delineate such as *storge*, which is akin to the love of a couple that has been married for a long time and who have grown into one soul. *Pragma*,

---

2. For information on faith as creed, see *Catechism of the Catholic Church* 167, 170–171; faith as a personal act, *CCC* 154–155, 166; faith as a grace, *CCC* 153.

mania, and *ludus* are still other forms of love. But in reference to God, *agape* is the appropriate form of religious love.

When we grow in both faith and love of God, the virtue of hope results. St. Faustina, the early twentieth-century Polish nun who received instructions from our Lord on the depths of his mercy, wrote, "I often ask the Lord Jesus for an intellect enlightened by faith. I express this to the Lord in these words. 'Jesus, give me an intellect, a great intellect, for this only, that I may understand You better; because the better I get to know You, the more ardently will I love You.'"[3] When these two virtues meet, hope and trust are the result. If faith is found primarily in the intellect and love in the will, hope is the virtue that encompasses our whole being and expresses itself in trust. In a sense, it is the most important virtue because it allows us to accept God's will, our daily sufferings and joys, and incorporate them into our relationship with God. Our Lord said to St. Faustina, "The graces of My mercy are drawn by means of one vessel only, and that is—trust. The more a soul trusts, the more it will receive. Souls that trust boundlessly are a great comfort to Me, because I pour all the treasures of My graces into them. I rejoice that they ask for much, because it is my desire to give much, very much."[4]

Almost three hundred years earlier, in the first half of the seventeenth century, at the dawn of the modern era, there was a man reminiscent of Thales of Miletus, the father of philosophy who we highlighted in chapter 3. Born in France, this man spent much of his life in the Netherlands. Like Thales, he was a philosopher, a scientist, and a mathematician. He is credited with linking algebra and geometry and forming the discipline of analytic geometry. He was a practicing Catholic and a student of Aristotle. And in his famous philosophical works, he systematically dismantled

---

3. Maria Faustina Kowalska, *Diary: Divine Mercy in My Soul* 1474, The Congregation of the Sisters of Our Lady of Mercy, https://www.saint-faustina.org/the-attitude-of-trust-in-god/?wide=true#more-63.

4. Kowalska, *Diary* 1578.

trust in our senses, in the world around us, and in God. Rather than trust, René Descartes introduced doubt. And in so doing, he became known as the Father of Modern Philosophy and gave birth to modern secular anthropology.

His famous phrase *Cogito, ergo sum* (I think, therefore I am) encapsulates his belief that the only thing that he can know and trust for certain is that he exists. The "I am" of Descartes stands in stark contrast to the great "I AM" of God's revelation to Moses. *Cogito, ergo sum* came to replace YHWH. Just like the serpent in the Garden, doubt was the tactic used to replace God. Just as the people at Babel sought to make a name for themselves without God, Descartes, perhaps inadvertently, made the human person the center and starting point of a new worldview. The rest of modern philosophy, literature, and history is humanity unpacking the consequences.

GOD IS DEAD, AND WE HAVE KILLED HIM

Friedrich Nietzsche famously proclaimed the death of belief in the existence of God. The rise of scientific rationalism during the Age of Enlightenment in the centuries after Descartes, he argued, had destroyed humanity's ability to trust in sacred revelation. Nietzsche knew that the death of God meant that we must bear the horrible responsibility of placing ourselves in God's place. In his work *The Joyful Wisdom*, he wrote, "God is dead! God remains dead! And we have killed him! How shall we console ourselves, the most murderous of all murderers? The holiest and the mightiest that the world has hitherto possessed, has bled to death under our knife,—who will wipe the blood from us? With what water could we cleanse ourselves? What lustrums, what sacred games shall we have to devise? Is not the magnitude of this deed too great for us? Shall we not ourselves have to become Gods, merely to seem worthy of it?"[5]

Nietzsche rigorously explored the impact of the principles laid down by Descartes and developed by philosophers of the eighteenth and nineteenth centuries. This led him to espouse the belief that objective truth and morals do not exist, and that existence itself is meaningless. More than doubt, it is a relativism that necessitates the rejection of all religious truth. Far from rejoicing at this development, Nietzsche was honest about the detrimental effects of nihilism, which he stated would lead to the rejection of faith and the greatest crisis in humanity. Considering the next century was by far the bloodiest in human history, it seems he was not wrong.

The tenets of nihilism are omnipresent in today's world. It is the air that surrounds us and that our children breathe. It is a silent killer, imperceptible and often undetectable. It is often present in literature, TV, and movies. It is the music that we listen to and the social media videos that appear on our phones. But the present storm and the violence and confusion of the past century were not unforeseeable or accidental. Nietzsche saw it and wrote about it clearly: "What I relate is the history of the next two centuries. I describe what is coming, what can no longer come differently: *the advent of nihilism.* . . . For some time now our whole European culture has been moving as toward a catastrophe, with a tortured tension that is growing from decade to decade: restlessly, violently, headlong, like a river that wants to reach the end."[6] What Descartes had started was growing into a full rejection of God's vision for the world and for the human person.

5. Friedrich Nietzsche, *The Joyful Wisdom,* aphorism 125, trans. Thomas Common (Edinburgh: T.N. Foulis, 1910), 168.

6. Friedrich Nietzsche, quoted in Alan Pratt, "Nihilism," Internet Encyclopedia of Philosophy, https://iep.utm.edu/nihilism/.

ERRORS SPREAD THROUGHOUT THE WORLD

On May 13, 1917, three young children were tending sheep in a field outside of a tiny village in Portugal. They had seen visions of an angel several times the previous year, but they were still unprepared when the beautiful lady, who seemed to be clothed with the sun, appeared to them that day. She asked the children to return every month on the thirteenth. During her visit in July, she told the children, "I shall come to the world to ask that Russia be consecrated to my Immaculate Heart, and I shall ask that on the First Saturday of every month Communions of reparation be made in atonement for the sins-of the world. If my wishes are fulfilled, Russia will be converted and there will be peace; if not, then Russia will spread her errors throughout the world, bringing new wars and persecution of the Church; the good will be martyred and the Holy Father will have much to suffer; certain nations will be annihilated. But in the end my Immaculate Heart will triumph."[7] The evil to which she alluded was the atheistic communism that was growing in Russia.

The year was a turbulent one in Russia. After a spontaneous uprising in February in St. Petersburg (which had recently been renamed Petrograd), Tsar Nicholas II abdicated from power, allowing for the formation of provisional governments. In April, Vladimir Lenin returned to Russia from exile and published his *April Theses*, ten directives that promoted and applied the concluding idea of Karl Marx and Friedrich Engels' *Communist Manifesto*: "Let the ruling classes tremble at a Communist revolution. The proletarians have nothing to lose but their chains. They have a world to win."[8] Lenin's ideas soon gained influence and provided direction to the revolution.

7. "Third Apparition of Our Lady," EWTN, https://www.ewtn.com/catholicism/devotions/third-apparition-of-our-lady-23365.
8. Karl Marx and Friedrich Engels, *Manifesto of the Communist Party*, trans. Samuel Moore (Chicago: Charles H. Kerr, 1910), 58.

In October, the Virgin Mary appeared on the thirteenth as promised for a final visit to the three children. Lucia Abobora, age ten, the oldest of the three visionaries, asked the lady, "I have many petitions from many people. Will you grant them?" With clarity and directness, she replied, "Some I shall grant, and others I must deny. People must amend their lives and ask pardon for their sins. They must not offend our Lord any more, for He is already too much offended!"[9] Shortly thereafter, all of those present witnessed a strange occurrence in which the sun appeared to move around the sky before seeming to fall upon the Earth. This event was witnessed by over seventy thousand and provided confirmation to those in attendance that the three children were indeed telling the truth about their heavenly visitor.

That same month, the Russian Revolution reached a climax with the murder of the Russian royal family and the formation of a Communist government led by Lenin. Over the next fifty years, atheistic communist governments in Russia and China would be responsible for the deaths of over seventy million of their own citizens. The consequences of a godless worldview were spreading throughout the world with a murderous insanity.[10]

THE CARDINAL PRINCIPLES OF SECONDARY EDUCATION

With the end of the First World War the following year, 1918, the American Commission on the Reorganization of Secondary Education issued a report to provide guidelines so that education could be intentional and uniform throughout the United States. Secondary education in the United States had been in disarray since the mid-nineteenth century. As society developed with an

---

9. "Sixth Apparition of Our Lady," EWTN, https://www.ewtn.com/catholicism /devotions/sixth-apparition-of-our-lady-23368.

10. For a complete history of the relationship of Fatima and the rise of communism in Russia, see Warren H. Carroll, *1917: Red Banners, White Mantle* (Front Royal, VA: Christendom Press, 1981).

increasingly secular understanding of the human person, it became more and more difficult to define the purpose of education. Not only was the rejection of Christian anthropology affecting world events on a massive scale; in a more subtle way, its impact was having a disorienting effect on American pedagogy and education.

While private and parochial education maintained more connection to the liberal arts tradition, the two main schools of thought for public education centered around college preparedness and vocational training. Any notion of the formation of the individual through a Christian understanding of the human person was off the table. In 1892, the National Education Association had tasked a group of educators, known as the Committee of Ten, to provide some guidance in this discussion. Their recommendations had favored college preparedness and kept elements of classical education as central but without any justification as to why, beyond the immediate needs of further study. Over twenty-five years later, and after seven years of deliberation, the Commission on the Reorganization for Secondary Education issued a report, *The Seven Cardinal Principles of Secondary Education*, based on the principles that education should be useful while acknowledging that what is useful is always changing. "Secondary education should be determined by the needs of the society to be served, the character of the individuals to be educated, and the knowledge of educational theory and practice available. These factors are by no means static."[11] The goal of education, the document states, should be guided by the principles of democracy and efficiency. Since society is always changing, education must continue to adapt to the needs of the individual. The theory and understanding of education itself was in flux, and the committee believed educational practices ought to adapt to new understandings.

11. Department of the Interior, Bureau of Education, *Cardinal Principles of Secondary Education: A Report of the Commission on the Reorganization of Secondary Education* (Washington, DC: Government Printing Office, 1918), 7, https://files.eric. ed.gov/fulltext/ED541063.pdf.

Oddly reminiscent of the seven liberal arts in structure, the "seven cardinal principles" were completely different in content, emphasizing health, being a worthy home member, ethical character development, appropriate leisure activities, civic education, and preparation to secure a livelihood. Only one of the seven principles, "command of fundamental process," was actually pedagogical, but even this was geared toward job preparedness. "There are various processes, such as reading, writing, arithmetical computations, and oral and written expression, that are needed as tools in the affairs of life. Consequently, command of these fundamental processes, while not an end in itself, is nevertheless an indispensable objective."[12] It is shocking to see how clearly unanchored the educational system had become. The committee investigating the issue seemed to acknowledge that they did not have any sense of how to ground their view of education in any ontological or essential reality of the human person.[13] As society lost its understanding of the human person, so also was the purpose of education lost.

"WINTER DREAMS"

One of the most common novels read in American secondary education today is F. Scott Fitzgerald's *The Great Gatsby*, with about half of all students in high school reading it at some point. Usually, the book is read as an American modern classic by one of our most distinguished authors. Lest anyone misunderstand me, let me be very clear: I do not like this book, and I think it falls short of the mark of classic literature. I dislike it for its equivocation: it showcases and promotes nihilism while pretending to disown and dislike it at the same time. Even more disturbing than the

12. *Cardinal Principles of Secondary Education*, 10.

13. For an introductory yet comprehensive analysis of the history of education, see Allan C. Ornstein and Daniel U. Levine, *Foundations of Education*, 10th ed. (Boston: Houghton Mifflin, 2008). There is a brief discussion about the Committee of Ten and the Commission for the Reorganization of Secondary Education on pages 138–139.

novel itself, however, is how it gets taught. Perhaps it is taught as an insight into the Roaring Twenties or an interesting study of the disappearance of the American dream, or possibly it is appreciated for its symbolism, such as the "all-seeing eye." But what teachers should be emphasizing if they do elect to read *The Great Gatsby* with their students is that this is what insipid and meaningless love looks like when shallow people try to fill their confused lives with some sense of godless purpose. If there is any lesson in *Gatsby*, that is the only one of any importance.

In short, *nouveau riche* Gatsby has always been in love with Daisy, who is now married to Tom. Tom is having an affair with Myrtle, who is married to George. Nick, Tom's friend from college, comes to town for the summer and watches as Tom hits Myrtle so hard he breaks her nose; Gatsby pines constantly and continuously over Daisy, the one thing he cannot have and truly wants; and Daisy accidentally runs over Myrtle while driving Gatsby's car. Tom implies to George that Gatsby was driving the car that killed his wife, so George shoots Gatsby, and Nick leaves Long Island revolted by the people with whom he has spent the summer. The main part of the story is Gatsby's infatuation with Daisy that has remained over the years.

Sometimes, in preparation for studying Gatsby, students read a short story by Fitzgerald called "Winter Dreams." It has the same theme as the novel and is seen as an earlier attempt to handle the ideas and narrative of *The Great Gatsby*. Dexter, a character that combines both the role of Nick the narrator and Gatsby, is a young caddy who becomes madly infatuated with Judy Jones, an arrogant, spoiled, manipulative version of Daisy. For years he is consumed by his desire for Judy, who toys with his affection as she does all her many suitors. Shortly before his engagement to Irene, he allows himself to be seduced by his former flame. Dexter has no regret when the repercussions of his actions lead to the end of his relationship with Irene and his reputation becomes compromised. The story concludes with a scene, seven years later, in which Dexter gets an update on Judy who has married and become a mother. Her husband is unfaithful, and she has become dull, her former good looks completely a thing of the past. The climax of the story finds Dexter despondent that Judy Jones is no longer beautiful. In the final words of the short story, he laments, "Long ago, long ago, there was something in me, but now that thing is gone. Now that thing is gone, that thing is gone. I cannot cry. I cannot care. That thing will come back no more."[14] Dexter demonstrates an experience of love that is transitory and superficial.

The most disturbing part of this whole narrative is that "Winter Dreams" is based on an infatuation and rejection Fitzgerald experienced personally a few years prior to writing the short story. He had fallen for a Chicago socialite, who treated him with scorn and indifference until he was publicly humiliated by the young woman's arrogant and wealthy father. *The Great Gatsby*, "Winter Dreams," and Fitzgerald's own experience are all a study in what love is not. The characters in all versions are vapid and shallow. They are led by feelings without any awareness of virtue or empathy, reason or vocation. They are emotionally immature and seemingly incapable of true sacrificial love. It is the secular vision of the human person on full display.

A COMMON SENSE SOLUTION

Gilbert Keith Chesterton was one of the sharpest minds of the twentieth century. C.S. Lewis credited his conversion to the writings of Chesterton. The well-known Thomistic philosopher Étienne Gilson stated that he was one of the most insightful thinkers of the age. Pope Pius XI gave him the title of "Defender of the Faith," making him only the second Englishman to receive that recognition.[15] Chesterton was a prolific author who explored

14. F. Scott Fitzgerald, "Winter Dreams," in *The Short Stories of F. Scott Fitzgerald: A New Collection*, ed. Matthew J. Bruccoli (New York: Scribner, 2003), 236.

15. Dale Ahlquist, *G.K. Chesterton: The Apostle of Common Sense* (San Francisco: Ignatius, 2003), 11, 17.

a vast array of topics with insight, wit, and acuity. But much of his work centered around exposing the illness of modern thought and providing the remedy of truth as found in the deposit of faith given to humanity by Christ. For Chesterton, this was just plain common sense. In the words of Dale Ahlquist, one of the foremost experts on the man and his writings, "Chesterton argued eloquently against materialism and scientific determinism, against relativism, agnosticism, atheism, and other diseased philosophies."[16] During his ministry to restore sanity to the world, Chesterton discovered that this deposit of faith has been entrusted to the Catholic Church, leading him to enter the Church in 1922 when he was almost fifty years old.

One characteristic of Chesterton is that his razor-sharp analysis of the world around him comes in paradoxical fashion. This can be seen in his assessment of modern society and its adherence to secular norms. "The modern world is not evil; in some ways the modern world is far too good."[17] The Christian virtues that dominated the cultural discussion in the age of Christendom are still alive and well, he states, albeit untethered. The modern ailment comes from the lack of coherence, and not from the absence, of virtue. "The modern world is full of the old Christian virtues gone mad. The virtues have gone mad because they have been isolated from each other and are wandering alone. Thus some scientists care for truth; and their truth is pitiless. Thus some humanitarians only care for pity; and their pity (I am sorry to say) is often untruthful."[18] This does not mean that his comments are free of a certain amount of sarcasm at times. "Those thinkers who cannot believe in any gods often assert that the love of humanity

16. Ahlquist, 12.

17. G.K. Chesterton, "The Suicide of Thought," in *Orthodoxy*. There is a new edition of Chesterton's seminal work with language adapted to the modern American reader. See *Orthodoxy: An American Translation*, ed. Dale Ahlquist, Peter Northcutt, and Kevin O'Brien (Hopkins, MN: ACS Books, 2020). The above citation is found on page 23.

18. Chesterton, *Orthodoxy*, 24.

would be in itself sufficient for them; and so, perhaps, it would, if they had it."[19]

Chesterton sought to counter the pessimism and doubt that modern nihilism has injected into the world by encouraging humanity to cultivate a sense of gratitude at the miracle of human existence. It is optimism and joy, says Chesterton, that allow humanity to rediscover a love of, and adherence to, truth and common sense. As one commentator puts it, "Like the difference between the existentialisms of Sartre and Kierkegaard, the prospect of human finitude may turn us either to despairing nihilism or to joyful faith. As if through the eyes of a child, Chesterton sees all things new, all things as wonderfully miraculous."[20] It is through this joy and optimism that we combat the heathen nihilism of old that has reappeared in our day, not in brutality and violence, but in the ideas of schools and lecture halls.[21]

This penetrating clarity with which Chesterton saw the world resulted at times in utterances that were near-prophetic in nature.[22] Twelve years before the rise of communism in Russia, Chesterton foretold both the rise and collapse of this godless system. Even more presciently, Chesterton warned that the greatest heresy of our time would not be the godless regime in Russia but the war on morality from secular society.[23] "The madness of tomorrow is not in Moscow but much more in Manhattan."[24] The rise of sexual promiscuity, which would "exalt lust and forbid fertility,"

19. G.K. Chesterton, "The Orthodox Barber," in *Tremendous Trifles* (New York: Dodd, Mead, and Co., 1909), 168.

20. Robert Moore-Jumonville, "Holding a Pistol to the Head of 'Modern Man': the Roots of G.K. Chesterton's Spiritual Theology," *Inklings Forever: Published Colloquium Proceedings 1997–2016* 6, no. 1 (2008), https://pillars.taylor.edu/cgi/viewcontent.cgi ?article=1150&context=inklings_forever.

21. For more on Chesterton's optimism, see Jared Zimmerer, "A Defense of Chestertonian Optimism," Word on Fire, December 4, 2020, https://www.wordonfire .org/articles/fellows/a-defense-of-chestertonian-optimism/, and Brian Gillen, *A Theology of Wonder: G.K. Chesterton's Response to Nihilism* (Leominster, UK: Gracewing, 2015).

22. Ahlquist, *Apostle of Common Sense*, 173.

23. Ahlquist, 175.

24. *G.K.'s Weekly*, June 19, 1926.

an obsession with diet and entertainment, and even the modern religious fervor surrounding sports were all foretold by Chesterton.[25] These insights also extended to the crisis in education that was unfolding in the Western world. "Obviously, it ought to be the oldest things that are taught to the youngest people; the assured and experienced truths that are put first to the baby. But in a school to-day the baby has to submit to a system that is younger than himself."[26]

Dorothy Sayers, the author of the essay "The Lost Tools of Learning," which became the catalyst for the modern revival of classical education as discussed in the introduction, was deeply influenced by Chesterton. "Thanks largely to Chesterton, Sayers's solution to the arbitrary absolutes and power of secular culture was the divine authority of Christian orthodoxy."[27] Indeed, it was Chesterton's book *Orthodoxy* that had helped her maintain her faith. Upon Chesterton's death, Sayers wrote to Frances, his wife of thirty-five years, stating that "G.K.'s books have become more a part of my mental make-up than those of any writer you could name."[28] Not only did Chesterton influence the woman recognized as the founder of the current revival of classical education, but his work and personal sanctity have inspired an entire network of classical Catholic schools that seek to educate students through his characteristic joy and optimism.

KNOWING AND LOVING

Seminarians from our archdiocese visit the Catholic high school where I work about once a year. Throughout the day, they address various religion classes, speaking on the importance of vocation,

25. Ahlquist, *Apostle of Common Sense*, 175–177.

26. G.K. Chesterton, "Authority the Unavoidable," in *What's Wrong with the World* (New York: Dodd, Mead, and Co., 1910), 255.

27. Crystal Downing, "Sayers 'Begins Here' with a Vision for Social and Intellectual Change," *Christian History Magazine* 113 (2015), https://christianhistoryinstitute.org/magazine/article/sayers-begins-here.

28. Downing, "Sayers."

sharing their witness, and answering questions. It is not an easy task for the seminarians. They have only a short time to convey how strongly and passionately they feel about serving the Lord and to educate the students about vocation to the priesthood and religious life.

One year, two seminarians addressed my juniors. One of them started with a broad and rather generic line: "Tell me what you know about God." There was an awkward silence that, in these situations, is not wholly unexpected. Broad questions about God can often elicit equally broad answers that lack theological depth and sophistication. But this awkward silence was different.

One of my students turned slightly and gave me a look seeking permission. I met her expression with one that said, "Sure, why not?" She raised her hand. The seminarian seemed relieved to break the silence and called on the young woman. "Are you asking about the sixteen attributes of God based on the teachings of St. Thomas Aquinas?" she asked. The seminarian was stunned and, looking to his colleague, said audibly that he was not sure and that he did not know that there were that many divine attributes. His honesty broke the tension and everyone relaxed. "Sure," he said, "tell me what you know." The student began to enumerate the divine attributes of God, making important distinctions between the different aspects of truth and how God is true in each sense of the word, as well as the different forms of justice and how God's justice to us is distributive. She talked for a while and then other students jumped in to fill in some information. The seminarians were stunned and asked the students questions. I stood in the back next to our campus minister who laughed when he saw me beaming with pride.

As stated earlier, it is not a secret that many young people are abandoning religion, including the Catholic faith. Consistently, one of the main reasons that young people give for their apostasy is that they no longer believe in the Church's teaching.[29] As a theology teacher, my issue with this problem is that the vast majority of these people likely do not know what the Church teaches with any amount of detail or accuracy. It is hard to accept that they have done an in-depth study of the *Catechism of the Catholic Church* before making their decision.[30] On the contrary, I have heard countless stories from those who have started to study the Church's teaching about their faith growing and becoming deeper.

This is why a comprehensive, detailed, and complete study of the faith should be done by all Catholics. This includes high schoolers. The United States Conference of Catholic Bishops has outlined the essential doctrinal elements that must be covered in a high school curriculum.[31] Many textbook companies take this into consideration when developing their materials.

But whenever possible, the classical classroom will avoid using the textbook as a middleman. The preference is always for the primary text. This means, in literature, to avoid prepackaged curricula that include excerpts of literary works, instead giving the students the actual book to read, annotate, discuss, and digest. The same holds true for discussions about philosophy and theology. Why use a textbook when you can read Plato's *Republic* or Aristotle's *Nicomachean Ethics*? Why not jump headfirst into Scripture and the *Catechism* as opposed to a text that talks about these vital books?

Beyond the exposure to the primary text, the classical classroom will go even further, asking students to internalize key concepts and definitions. Theology students build a vocabulary

29. Brandon Vogt, "New Stats on Why Young People Leave the Church," https://brandonvogt.com/new-stats-young-people-leave-church/.

30. Nicolette Manglos-Weber and Christian Smith, "Understanding Former Young Catholics," McGrath Institute for Church Life at the University of Notre Dame website, https://mcgrath.nd.edu/assets/170517/icl_former_catholics_final_web.pdf.

31. United States Conference of Catholic Bishops, "Doctrinal Elements of a Curriculum Framework for the Development of Catechetical Materials for Young People of High School Age," USCCB website, https://www.usccb.org/beliefs-and-teachings/how-we-teach/catechesis/upload/high-school-curriculum-framework.pdf.

that respects the rigorous and intellectually stimulating deposit of faith that has been handed down to us as well as the theological discussion that has sought to contemplate these eternal truths.

Every Catholic school should want to do this with their theology classes. Some do, some do not. Classical Catholic high schools on the whole tend to place this emphasis on theological knowledge. Nothing can better prepare the student for the personal encounter with the Lord than a deep immersion into the truth of God's revelation. Students in the classical program that I direct receive the same weighting for their theology class as an Advanced Placement College Board class. This is not surprising to them since they can see firsthand that the workload is similarly demanding. In addition, the students have the opportunity to use their knowledge in the classroom to earn college credit for their knowledge of the *Catechism*.[32]

The answer to the current crisis of faith that is being experienced by our teens and young adults will ultimately be one of love. But as St. Thomas and countless others have taught centuries before our modern plight, the heart cannot love what the mind does not know.[33]

BE NOT AFRAID

Secular anthropology is a lie. Just like the first deception in the Garden, it starts by planting seeds of doubt. It tells us that we do not need God, that we can be our own god. But it does not make good on any of its promises. It assures us that we ought to self-actualize and assert our individuality and our autonomy. Instead, it causes us to experience isolation, confusion, and hopelessness. It was the first lie. It is the great lie. And it is the lie that permeates our culture and surrounds us and our children. Teenagers today are often characterized as sullen or arrogant or

32. See "Franciscan Advantage," Franciscan University of Steubenville, https://franciscan.edu/advantage/.
33. See Thomas Aquinas, *Summa theologiae* 2-2.27.1.

withdrawn or cantankerous, but this is not who they are or who they are called to be. St. Francis, St. Thomas, St. Catherine of Siena, St. Thérèse of Lisieux, and St. Joan of Arc were all teenagers when they opened themselves to the radical love of God. Carlo Acutis was fifteen when he died in 2006 and has been declared "Blessed" by the Church.

Another great saint of the Church who embraced the call to holiness at a young age was Karol Wojtyła. The spiritual influences on the early life of the future Pope St. John Paul II are well documented, from the importance of the example of his father to his high school drama teacher. As Father, Bishop, and Cardinal Wojtyła, and later as Pope John Paul II, he had a great understanding of the importance of the spiritual development of young people and the role of education. In a very real sense, his life's work and mission can be summarized as exposing the lies of secular anthropology and a call to return to the Christian anthropology of the Gospel. George Weigel, the biographer of the pope, commented, "The task of education, John Paul II would insist, is to lift us out of the slough of skepticism and relativism and into the bright uplands of the truth. Educators best do that, he would add, by being attentive to both the life of the mind and the life of the soul."[34]

Throughout his pontificate, he addressed young people and repeated the central challenge of Christianity. In an address to high school students in 1979, he said, "Only in Christ do we find real love, and the fullness of life. And so I invite you today to look to Christ. When you wonder about the mystery of yourself, look to Christ who gives you the meaning of life."[35] The consistent message throughout Pope John Paul II's pontificate is synonymous with the

34. George Weigel, "The Educational Pilgrimage of St. John Paul II and Its Impact on the World," *Catholic World Report*, February 22, 2021, https://www.catholicworld report.com/2021/02/22/the-educational-pilgrimage-of-st-john-paul-ii-and-its-impact-on -the-world/.

35. John Paul II, "Address of His Holiness John Paul II to High School Students" 2, October 3, 1979, vatican.va.

goal of classical Catholic education, for both are consistent with the message of the Gospel. It is not that John Paul's message was new; it was that people were living in a world that had forgotten the radical call of Christ. In 1996, he declared, "True holiness does not mean a flight from the world; rather, it lies in the effort to incarnate the Gospel in everyday life, in the family, at school and at work, and in social and political involvement."[36] And at World Youth Day during the great Jubilee of 2000, he declared,

> It is Jesus in fact that you seek when you dream of happiness; he is waiting for you when nothing else you find satisfies you; he is the beauty to which you are so attracted; it is he who provokes you with that thirst for fullness that will not let you settle for compromise; it is he who urges you to shed the masks of a false life; it is he who reads in your hearts your most genuine choices, the choices that others try to stifle. It is Jesus who stirs in you the desire to do something great with your lives, the will to follow an ideal, the refusal to allow yourselves to be grounded down by mediocrity, the courage to commit yourselves humbly and patiently to improving yourselves and society, making the world more human and more fraternal.[37]

In his 1998 encyclical, *Fides et Ratio* (*Faith and Reason*), which has so much in common with the essence and aim of classical Catholic education, the pope urged people to rediscover and acknowledge the unity and harmony that exists between faith and reason. The famous opening lines employ a metaphor reminiscent of Plato's example of a chariot pulled by horses in the dialogue *Phaedrus*: "Faith and reason are like two wings on

36. John Paul II, "Message of his Holiness John Paul II to Participants in the Seventh International Meeting of the 'Catholic Fraternity of Covenant Communities and Fellowships'" 4, November 9, 1996, vatican.va.

37. John Paul II, "Address of the Holy Father John Paul II: 15th World Youth Day Vigil of Prayer" 5, August 19, 2000, vatican.va.

which the human spirit rises to the contemplation of truth; and God has placed in the human heart a desire to know the truth—in a word, to know himself—so that, by knowing and loving God, men and women may also come to the fullness of truth about themselves."[38] The Holy Father was acutely aware of the dangers of secular anthropology and nihilism and addressed in clear language the hazards they present: "Quite apart from the fact that it conflicts with the demands and the content of the word of God, *nihilism* is a denial of the humanity and of the very identity of the human being."[39] Embracing and promoting a metaphysical and transcendental worldview that is central to classical Catholic education, he continued,

> It should never be forgotten that the neglect of being inevitably leads to losing touch with objective truth and therefore with the very ground of human dignity. This in turn makes it possible to erase from the countenance of man and woman the marks of their likeness to God, and thus to lead them little by little either to a destructive will to power or to a solitude without hope. Once the truth is denied to human beings, it is pure illusion to try to set them free. Truth and freedom either go together hand in hand or together they perish in misery.[40]

It is worth noting that the introduction to this encyclical bears the title "Know Yourself."

It is not surprising that the worldview put forward by St. John Paul II is identical with the vision of classical Catholic education and its pedagogy, for he himself was a product of classical Catholic education.[41] Growing up in the small town of Wadowice, the young Karol Wojtyła excelled in the study of both Latin and

38. John Paul II, *Fides et Ratio*, encyclical letter, September 14, 1998, vatican.va.
39. *Fides et Ratio* 90.
40. *Fides et Ratio* 90.
41. Weigel, "Educational Pilgrimage of St. John Paul II."

Greek. His educational program assumed the liberal arts as the only viable template for education. Memorization, recitations, and rigorous catechetical instruction were taken as obvious and essential pedagogical tools. Shortly after his ordination, he served as chaplain to the university students of Krakow, organizing small study groups to read and discuss some of the great classical and Christian texts in Socratic fashion.[42]

Having been a teacher himself as well as a moral philosophy professor at the Catholic University of Lublin, John Paul II understood the awesome responsibility and calling of the Catholic school educator. "The life of a teacher, as I know from personal experience, is very challenging and demanding, but it is also profoundly satisfying. It is more than a job, for it is rooted in our deepest convictions and values. To be intimately concerned in the development of a young person, of hundreds of young people, is a highly responsible task."[43] This is why the job of a teacher can only be properly understood as a vocation, a calling. Early on I said that teaching was a craft and that educators were artists. The lives of their students are their canvases. They can do tremendous good (or harm) by their influence on the lives of those they teach. If a Catholic school is to succeed in its mission, the faculty must bring the Gospel message of Christ to life in the classroom. They must create environments where students can encounter the love of Christ. "As teachers," John Paul II explained, "you kindle in your students a thirst for truth and wisdom. You spark off in them a desire for beauty. You introduce them to their cultural heritage. You help them to discover the treasures of other cultures and peoples. What an awesome responsibility and privilege is yours in the teaching profession."[44] Perhaps the clearest espousal of Christian anthropology in education can be found in his address to a group

42. Weigel, "Educational Pilgrimage of St. John Paul II."

43. John Paul II, "Address of John Paul II to the Council, Staff and Students of the Institute of Catholic Education" 2, November 28, 1986, vatican.va.

44. "Address of John Paul II to the Council, Staff, and Students" 2.

of American bishops in which he said, "Catholic education aims not only to communicate facts, but also to transmit a coherent, comprehensive vision of life, in the conviction that the truths contained in that vision liberate students in the most profound meaning of human freedom."[45]

Cardinal Karol Wojtyła was elected pope on October 16, 1978. On Sunday, October 22, he addressed the Church from St. Peter's Square at the Vatican for the inauguration of his pontificate and encouraged the faithful, "Be not afraid!" During this first address, he showed a clear understanding of the responsibility we have as pilgrims, parents, educators, and students in this modern era: "So often today man does not know what is within him, in the depths of his mind and heart. So often he is uncertain about the meaning of his life on this earth. He is assailed by doubt, a doubt which turns into despair. We ask you therefore, we beg you with humility and trust, let Christ speak to man. He alone has words of life, yes, of eternal life."[46] Two and a half years later, on May 13, 1981, the anniversary of the first apparition of Our Lady of Fatima, the Holy Father was shot by an attempted assassin in St. Peter's Square. He attributed his survival to her intercession. Over the next two decades, the Holy Father would help bring about an end to communism in Russia and shepherd the Church into the third millennium. His message could not be silenced, and he continued to preach trust, love, and holiness to the world, focusing especially on the youth. "Do not be satisfied with mediocrity. . . . Do not be afraid to be holy! Have the courage and humility to present your-selves to the world determined to be holy, since full, true freedom is

45. John Paul II, "Address of the Holy Father Pope John Paul II to the Bishops of the Ecclesiastical Regions of Chicago, Indianapolis and Milwaukee (USA) on Their 'Ad Limina' Visit" 3, May 30, 1998, vatican.va.

46. John Paul II, "Homily of His Holiness John Paul II for the Inauguration of His Pontificate" 5, October 22, 1978, vatican.va.

born from holiness. This aspiration will help you discover genuine love, untainted by selfish and alienating permissiveness."[47]

SUMMARY

At some point around the fifteenth century, the harmony of faith and secular life began to weaken. Some attribute it to the effect of the Crusades or the Black Death, but there are traces in literature of a sinister internal malaise. In *The Canterbury Tales*, we see a cultural Christendom that lacks the inner relationship with God that is necessary to sustain and grow a culture of faith and harmony. Several tales told by the pilgrims are lewd and offensive. This is not the case of the Pardoner's Tale, whose story is deep and poignant. It is the life of the Pardoner, who unapologetically deals in simony by selling false relics, that betrays a sickness in Christendom. And this illness would soon give way to disease.

We saw the importance of the spirituality of the two ways in chapter 2. We are either in a relationship with Christ and open to the grace he offers, or we have shut ourselves to the divine and God's indwelling presence. The same dynamic holds true for our understanding of the human person: either we allow God's revelation to form our anthropology, or we define ourselves apart from God. René Descartes introduced methodological doubt into the philosophical dialogue. This doubt impacted our relationship with all objective reality, from God to the ability to trust our senses, and left us with a certainty in ourselves alone. From doubt quickly came skepticism, and from skepticism arose atheism. As the secular anthropology of modern philosophy continued down the spiral of a world divorced from the defining love of God, humanity soon found itself confronted by a life devoid of meaning and purpose.

47. John Paul II, "Message of the Holy Father to Youth Meeting in Santiago de Compostela" 3, August 7, 1999, vatican.va.

Although perhaps not apparent at the time, the logical conclusion of this displacement was not only a distrust but a contempt for the world and the truth that surrounds us. Nihilism is the natural conclusion of secular anthropology, and the philosophical world reached that conclusion within a few hundred years. It is no surprise that, as the world rejected God, cataclysmic war and unprecedented killing were the result. Lest anyone think that the rise of godlessness and the evils of the mass murders of the twentieth century are unrelated, the apparition of Our Lady to three uneducated and very young shepherds in Portugal makes the connection remarkably clear. The year of the apparition, 1917, was also the year of the Communist Revolution in Russia, and the connection between the two events is startling.

This existential confusion also impacted the history of education. In the United States, those in charge of the public school system in the late nineteenth and early twentieth centuries were openly at a loss as to the goal and reason for secondary education. Their attempts to provide a rationale were self-admittedly very weak.

In our present day, nihilism is on full display, and unabashedly and unapologetically so, but in the twentieth century, people were still apprehensive about fully committing to a worldview that confessed that the world was vapid and pointless. The ubiquitous high school novel *The Great Gatsby* and the story upon which it was based give evidence to a world where love is misunderstood and humanity has become unmoored. Amidst this upheaval, G.K. Chesterton and Pope St. John Paul II emerged as defenders of truth who exposed the shallowness of secular anthropology. Chesterton's voice was one of common sense and prophetic clarity; his penetrating insight provided a response before the modern world had realized the question it was asking. And few people have understood the shallow lies of secular anthropology better than Pope St. John Paul II. The main focus of his pontificate was to expose those lies and to call humanity back to the beauty of

Christian anthropology. In rediscovering God's intent and design for the human person, we can embrace our dignity and purpose as sons and daughters of the Father. A former teacher himself, John Paul II speaks powerfully on the role of teachers and the importance of education in helping our youth to see themselves as loved by the Father.

Conclusion

It must have been a Friday. I should have seen it coming, but I was still surprised. When I arrived home from school one day in May during sixth grade, my mom announced that we were moving to Belgium. Part of this was understandable: my dad worked for the military as a civil servant, so we moved every three years, and since we had been living in Massachusetts for three years, I should have known that a move was coming. People often feel the need to express sympathy when I tell them how often we moved, but I actually enjoyed it. After a few relocations (this was my sixth), I was starting to get the hang of it: first year, difficult; second year, good; third year, great, never want to leave. Then we would move. The advantage was that I had friends all over the country and soon from all over the world. So I should have known the announcement was coming. But Belgium was a surprise.

My mom is from the Netherlands, so, to a certain extent, it made sense. We would get a chance to be close to her family and see where she grew up. But even though we had family there, it felt completely unknown. I remember that I went straight to the mobile library van that parked up the street every other Friday (that is how I know it must have been a Friday) and found a book on Belgium. I sat on the carpeted floor of the converted bus and started to read. I still remember the first sentence: "In Belgium, it rains around two hundred days a year . . ."

Despite the rain, my four years in Belgium were an incredible experience. I chose to go to a French-speaking school (even though I didn't speak French) instead of the American one on the base. I took Dutch as a second language after a failed attempt at Latin. I made great friends from all over the world. My best friends ended up being Portuguese and Dutch (and Belgian, of course). Living in a foreign country was an eye-opening experience that I would recommend to anyone, and I think that just living overseas was as much of an education in some respects as being in school. But in terms of my moral development, it was a disaster. All of the typical high school temptations seemed to start earlier in Belgium. And by the time I left at the end of tenth grade, I had developed an impressive repertoire of not just sins but firmly rooted vices.

Of all the moves I have made, coming back to the States and entering eleventh grade in an American high school in the eighties was the most difficult. It was a miserable year, and I had met a crowd of people who were able to help me expand and cement my vices even more. By the summer before senior year, I was thoroughly steeped in a world of depravity that, even though it had promised me great happiness, produced nothing but misery, loneliness, and constant inner pain. The fact that the same people who told me sex, drugs, and rock and roll were all that I ever wanted also bemoaned that they could not get any satisfaction should have been a clue. But I had bought the lie of secular anthropology wholeheartedly, and it was killing me.

It must have been a Tuesday in September of my senior year of high school, since I worked nearly every day except Tuesday. There is a lot about that evening I do not remember. But at some point, for whatever reason, I was standing in my room. I was wearing a black sweater and holding a piece of paper—I have no idea why or what was on it, but I remember it falling to the floor. That moment is in my memory at all times, every day. I think back to it continuously. It was like a flood of light, a giant rush from above that inundated me, filled me, overwhelmed me. As I stood there,

I was overcome with an awareness of the Father's love. Perhaps it was just a fraction of what we experience in heaven; perhaps it was exactly what we feel in heaven. I have no way of comparing it—it was like nothing I had ever experienced or have since. It was a profound, intense awareness of the Father loving me—not for anything that I had done, but on the contrary, in spite of what I had done. It was more real than anything I have ever experienced; it is impossible to deny. I know that he exists. I am more certain of it than the world around me every day or anything else that has ever happened.

It was an experience of the delight the Father has when he looks at me. It was beyond happiness. It ravished my soul, and it changed my entire life. From that moment, I had to search for him, to find him, to try to love him, to serve him. The next day, with no reason or explanation, I became friends with an entirely different group at school, people who had known each other since kindergarten. This does not happen in high school. All of a sudden, we were walking down the halls laughing and joking together. I remember one of them turning around and saying, "How do I even know you?" I laughed and thought to myself, "You wouldn't believe me if I told you!" Those friends are still with me to this day. They were good people. We did homework after school and did fun, wholesome activities together. They tried to get me to stop smoking (something I started in seventh grade). Slowly, because of their good example, I was giving up on my vices. I was infinitely happier.

Later, after I had continued to grow and heal at a Catholic liberal arts college, some of us in the friend group started to seriously look into the spiritual life. We began fasting on Fridays and going to Adoration. We would read books on spiritual growth and talk about theology until late at night. Two of my friends ended up entering the seminary and became priests. But for me, it all started that Tuesday night in September in my room. I have no idea how long that experience of God's love lasted—probably just a few seconds—but it has reverberated through the years. That moment is the reason that I ended up working with high school students and telling them over and over that there is a loving God waiting to be encountered. It is what he wants me to do. It must have been his plan all along.

EUDAIMONIA VS. EUPHORIA

I am not a fan of the show *Euphoria*. Admittedly, I am not the target audience. But I do not base my dislike just on how crude, violent, or hypersexualized the show is. In a certain sense, I appreciate all the horrible stuff: the drug abuse, the meaningless sex, the lack of self-esteem, the unhappiness of the characters, the main protagonist being a violent sociopath. Even though it is ridiculous to pretend that these characters, who are far more depraved than most high schoolers and portrayed by actors who are nowhere near the age of actual teenagers, represent the experience of most adolescents, the show does admit to representing the meaninglessness of secular anthropology. And it is true: the lives of the characters are devoid of truth, goodness, and beauty. They are empty, shallow, and vapid. Their lives have no point and no meaning beyond the desperate hope for a minute of happiness here and there. These are people without God. They do not understand themselves through the love of God. In fact, they do not understand themselves at all. Unlike *The Great Gatsby*, which tries to be both for and against the modern existential crisis, *Euphoria* is the emptiness of nihilism on full display, without any apology or excuse. I appreciate the show's honesty.

Before the birth of Christ, humanity was on a path that was leading toward the Incarnation. There was even a sense of longing and anticipation in the world. When the Son of God entered the human drama by becoming man and redeeming us through his sacrifice on the cross, all of history and culture was changed. Slowly, over the centuries, the impact of the Incarnation transformed human society. Reason and faith worked together in ever-increasing harmony. In a sense, the Christian worldview can be summarized by this word: harmony. Having a strong, healthy, vibrant relationship with God, with our family, with the world around us, is the harmony for which we were created. This is what we lost in the Garden by the tree, and this is what was regained when Christ redeemed us on the cross.

This Christian worldview presents a vision of the human person as understood through the love of our Creator and Redeemer. It shows us how good and important we are and how much dignity we have as sons and daughters of the Father. It is a world of beauty and truth where people strive to be the best version of themselves, not out of vanity or overcompensation for low self-esteem, but because we know ourselves to be loved and called to a life of excellence, a life that Aristotle called *eudaimonia*. And it is the polar opposite of euphoria.

FROM THALES TO ARISTOTLE

One of the greatest works of Aristotle is a book called the *Nicomachean Ethics*. It was a work on discovering how to live a happy life and was written by Aristotle, possibly as a guide for his son, Nicomachus. It is especially fitting to end this discussion with a book by one of our great philosophical guides written for his teenage son. There is something tender in thinking about this great philosopher writing a manual to help his son embrace the fullness that life has to offer. Perhaps this is why the book has such a tremendous impact on high school students.

The subject of the *Nicomachean Ethics* is how to live a happy life. More than nearly everyone in the ancient world except the Hebrew prophets, Aristotle had a sense of the beauty of life and of the divine hand in creation. He also had a theory about what our lives ought to be like. We are to strive for virtue in all things, he states, in order to live well and attain *eudaimonia*, a Greek word often translated as well-being, happiness, or human flourishing. On a human level, it is what compels us to strive for excellence and be averse to mediocrity. It is a life of personal excellence and excellence of character. It is how we are called to live.

In his treatise, Aristotle teaches that people achieve excellence of character through a life of virtue. He argues that someone who possesses personal excellence does the right thing, at the right time, and in the right way. Moderation, kindness toward others, and self-control are examples of character excellence or virtue. Each of these traits exists on a continuum. The span of the continuum admits of both a deficiency on one end and an excess of that trait on the other. In the middle, between the two, lies the golden mean, the proper amount, and this is what Aristotle calls virtue. For example, too much confidence means one is rash. Too little of this trait is cowardice. And in the middle lies the virtue of courage. This is how all virtue needs to be cultivated: finding the right amount to be applied at the right time in the right way. Additionally, Aristotle teaches that the right way to act depends upon the circumstances. This was the essence of virtue, a type of practical wisdom that understands the right thing to do in every situation. But, despite the importance of practical decision-making, Socrates, Plato, and Aristotle all agree that if we are to live our best life, we must also embrace the metaphysical and transcendental worldview that comes from study.

In order to live a life of *eudaimonia*, Aristotle teaches that one must develop intellectual virtue and not only practical virtue. "If happiness is activity in accord with virtue, it is reasonable for it to accord with the supreme virtue, which will be the virtue of the best thing . . . and we have said that this activity is the activity of study."[1] A person searching to live a life of flourishing will cultivate virtue, and the ability to lead such a life will come through experience but primarily through reflection and study.

---

1. Aristotle, *Nicomachean Ethics* 10.7, 2nd ed., trans. Terence Irwin (Indianapolis: Hackett, 1999), 163.

This is the highest form of life: cultivating an attitude of self-knowledge and thoughtful reflection on what is true, beautiful, and good. This happens through the pursuit and acquisition of knowledge. "For what is proper to each thing's nature is supremely best and most pleasant for it; and hence for a human being the life in accord with understanding will be supremely best and most pleasant. . . . This life, then, will also be happiest."[2] Since we are rational creatures by nature, the cultivation of our reason will not only help us achieve happiness in the future but also in the current moment. It will help us attain *eudaimonia*.

But Aristotle does not stop there in his praise of learning. Not only is the pursuit of knowledge the highest activity that we can do as humans; it carries within it a spark of the divine. "Such a life [of study] would be superior to the human level. For someone will live it not insofar as he is a human being, but insofar as he has some divine element in him."[3] Therefore, as we learn and participate in education, we connect with that within us that is divine, what the Greeks and early Christians so often termed the *Logos*, the Word of God. "In the beginning was the Word, and the Word was with God, and the Word was God. He was in the beginning with God. All things came into being through him, and without him not one thing came into being. What has come into being in him was life, and the life was the light of all people" (John 1:1–4). The life of flourishing, the life of virtue, the life of learning, the life of understanding, the life of grace—this is our call as humans and as sons and daughters of God the Father. "Hence if understanding is something divine in comparison with a human being, so also will the life in accord with understanding be divine in comparison with human life."[4]

This is the goal of classical Catholic education: the discovery, through an integrated study of truth and reality, of the divine life

2. *Nicomachean Ethics* 10.7, 165.
3. *Nicomachean Ethics* 10.7, 164.
4. *Nicomachean Ethics* 10.7, 164.

within and the call to be the fullest, most complete, most authentic versions of ourselves. It is a life of harmony and of grace. And in order to live this life of *eudaimonia*, you must strive to discover who you are and what you are called to become. You must learn to know thyself.

Further Reading

The world of classical Catholic education is rich and vast. It encompasses the great literature that humanity has produced, as well as the totality of science, math, music, art, history, and philosophy. Those entering into the world of classical Catholic education have all of knowledge before them. But for those interested in learning more, where does one start? The following list offers suggestions for parents and educators for further resources and reading recommendations. For ongoing book recommendations and suggestions on classical Catholic education and pedagogy, follow me on Instagram at classicalcatholicteacher. For information about speaking, consulting, and training, contact me through linktr.ee/andrewyoungblood.

CLASSICAL CATHOLIC RESOURCES

For those wishing to read further, *Beauty in the Word: Rethinking the Foundations of Education* by Stratford Caldecott offers an in-depth examination of the trivium and how it applies to education. It contains more information about the elementary years.

The Holy See's Teaching on Catholic Schools by Archbishop J. Michael Miller, CSB, offers a summary of recent Church writings on education. Although not classical, this brief and concise work is an important foundational read for parents and educators.

The Case for Catholic Education by Ryan N.S. Topping is a favorably peer-reviewed examination of the purpose of Catholic education. The assumption that Catholic pedagogy is, in essence, classical is overt in this work.

For those interested in starting a classical Catholic high school, the Chesterton Schools Network (CSN) provides a comprehensive program for all facets of the school-founding process, including toolkits for fundraising, board formation guidance, and an eighteen-month guided startup process. Additionally, the CSN provides a complete and comprehensive integrated curriculum with daily lesson plans and teacher training as well as ongoing formation for heads of school. For more information, visit https:// chestertonschoolsnetwork.org. I have served as the Director of Curriculum and Instruction for the network since 2017 and have witnessed its explosive growth.

The Institute for Catholic Liberal Education (ICLE) "was founded in 1999 to help educators renew today's Catholic schools by drawing on the Church's tradition," according to their website.[1] The ICLE offers training for teachers and administrators.

Renewing Catholic Schools: How to Regain a Catholic Vision in a Secular Age, edited by R. Jared Staudt, offers a collection of essays by leaders in the classical Catholic movement, many associated with ICLE. Mary Pat Donoghue, Executive Director for the Secretariat of Education for the United States Conference of Catholic Bishops, states, "This insightful and inspiring work provides a roadmap for Catholic educators and parents seeking to reform and renew Catholic education by turning fully to the Church's own understanding of education."

The University of Dallas, through the Braniff Graduate School, offers a master's degree in classical education. According to the website:

---

1. Institute for Catholic Liberal Education website, "Our Story," https://catholic liberaleducation.org/our-story/.

By providing foundations in classical principles and pedagogy, the Classical Education Graduate Program aspires to form educators as master teachers. Students in the program explore the historical, philosophic, literary, aesthetic, rhetorical, and scientific roots of the liberal arts in the Western tradition. With a dedicated faculty and staff drawing on extensive experience in the academy and the classical classroom, and assisted by UD's world-class undergraduate faculty, the Classical Education Graduate Program combines the ethos of the university's core curriculum tradition with a concentration on the theory and practice of classical education, bringing these to working and aspiring classical school teachers, school administrators, and others both locally and around the country.[2]

NON-CATHOLIC CLASSICAL RESOURCES

Offering perhaps the highest-quality resources, Hillsdale College Online Courses are free and open to all. These courses are an amazing resource. For those wishing to enter the world of classical literature and learning for their own personal growth, I recommend beginning the journey with the course on the *Divine Comedy*, a breathtakingly beautiful work presented in an equally edifying manner. For those interested in teacher training and school resources, Hillsdale also offers a K–12 Education Office that, according to the website, "teaches schools and communities about the principles of excellent K–12 education, focusing on board governance, school leadership, curriculum, classroom instruction, and school culture."[3] As a third resource, the Hillsdale Graduate School for Classical Education offers a master's degree in classical studies.

2. "Classical Education Graduate Program," Braniff Graduate School at the University of Dallas website, https://udallas.edu/braniff/academics/ma/classical _education/.

3. Hillsdale College website, https://k12.hillsdale.edu/.

The Liberal Arts Tradition: A Philosophy of Christian Classical Education by Ravi Scott Jain and Kevin Clark is one of the best resources for a thorough and well-researched discussion on the topic of classical education. It also includes extensive footnotes for those wishing to delve further into the study of the liberal arts. Some of the discussions might be challenging for the novice at times, and the presentation does not grasp the fullness of truth present in the Catholic faith and sacraments.

An Introduction to Classical Education: A Guide For Parents by Dr. Christopher Perrin is a short forty-eight-page booklet that is accessible and engaging.

Both of the titles above, along with many others, are published by Classical Academic Press, a great resource for classical material and study. They also offer ClassicalU, an online platform with over seventy courses for teachers and parents.

Discussion Questions

1. Reflect on your own education. How would you describe your high school experience? What helped you the most to grow academically and spiritually and to develop as a person?

2. Nearly everyone goes to high school. But why? What would you say is the purpose of high school? How would you describe the common traits of students who are entering their freshman year, and what do you think they should have accomplished in terms of personal growth by the time they graduate?

CHAPTER 1: EDUCATION

1. How would you describe your child's educational journey so far? What do you think are areas of strengths and areas of improvement? Has your child been successful in school, or has it been a struggle? Does your child find joy in learning?

2. Everything that happens in education is an extension of what happens at home. *The Catechism of the Catholic Church* teaches, "Parents have the first responsibility for the education of their children. They bear witness to this responsibility first by creating a home where tenderness, forgiveness, respect, fidelity, and disinterested service are the rule." What have you done to create a home that emphasizes and encourages

learning—not for the sake of grades but because it is vital that we continue to learn throughout life? Do you as a family make daily time for reading?

3. Forgiveness is an important part of every relationship. As a family, have you prioritized the regular reception of the sacrament of Penance? How do you generally forgive one another in your family?

CHAPTER 2: CATHOLIC EDUCATION

1. The home is called the domestic church. What do you do to bring the faith alive on a daily basis in your home? Do you prioritize Mass on weekends and daily prayer?

2. What are the choices for high school in your local area? Rate each school based on your perception of how well it will form your child academically, spiritually, and in character development. What are the realistic financial options available to you?

3. What graces have you experienced in your faith journey? Have you shared these moments with your family? Where are you in your journey with Christ?

CHAPTER 3: CLASSICAL CATHOLIC EDUCATION

1. An essential aspect of classical education is that it integrates all of learning into one narrative. What connections do you see between the different disciplines offered in high school? How are they related? Are there some classes that do not seem related at all?

2. It is very common for high schoolers, when referring to any number of subjects from calculus or geometry to literature, to complain, "Why am I learning this?" How would you answer

this question? What is the purpose of learning "non-useful" things? Why are the fine arts an essential part of a high school education?

3. Education can and should be transformative. How were you transformed by your educational journey in high school? What do you wish you had done differently? How has your education helped you to be a better, more complete person?

4. Have you ever experienced a discussion-based learning environment that was guided by the teacher but led by the students? College seminars, book clubs, and faith-sharing groups all have a similar format. What do you think are the benefits of this learning environment?

5. A fundamental difference between nonclassical and classical pedagogy is the purpose of education. To what extent do you want high school to prepare your child for a college/job/ career, and to what extent do you expect high school to help transform your child into a better version of himself, equipped to handle the challenges and joys of adult life?

CHAPTER 4:
THE ANCIENT WORLD: LONGING FOR CHRIST

1. Classical education often follows a historical sequence. What is the benefit of this model? How does this format reflect and respect the pedagogical approach that God adopts with humanity? What are the benefits of providing a narrative approach to classes, school years, and the high school experience in general?

2. Longing for peace, redemption, or resolution is a common theme in literature and an essential component to the conflict/ resolution model to storytelling. What is your favorite example from a book or movie of a character finding peace or finding

redemption? What does this character development entail? What challenges did the character face, and how does the conclusion of their search transform them?

3. The Church teaches that we can come to discover the existence of God through reason. Read paragraphs 31 through 35 in the *Catechism of the Catholic Church*, and discuss how people can come to know God through their experiences of the created world.

CHAPTER 5:
THE INCARNATION: CHRISTIAN ANTHROPOLOGY

1. The process of learning is complex and fascinating. What is your reaction to the analogy of learning being like childbirth? And what are your thoughts on the image of the teacher as a midwife? How does this idea about learning transform our approach to pedagogy? What are the potential drawbacks in a lecture-based learning environment? What safeguards would need to be adopted to ensure that lecture-based learning is connecting with the student?

2. We are all on a search for happiness. This search is especially important for high school students as they experience great change and growth in their lives. How would you explain what happiness is and how to attain it? Have these "bigger questions" about life arisen in your family conversations? How can you encourage your family to have these discussions about happiness, purpose, and friendship? How can you encourage conversation with your children about God's presence and activity in our daily lives?

3. The Church teaches that the celebration of the Eucharist is the source and summit of our faith. How is the encounter with Christ in the Eucharist the source and origin of our faith?

How is it the summit and culmination of our relationship with God?

CHAPTER 6:
CHRISTENDOM: SCHOLARS AND SAINTS

1. Who is your favorite saint? How do the saints help as our models of faith and intercessors? How does our participation in the communion of saints help us on our faith journey?

2. The teenage years can be challenging for children and parents alike. What are some of your favorite parts about parenting teenagers? What are the struggles? How would you describe the path of gradual independence for a young adult? What are the stages of gradual independence? How will you navigate this changing relationship?

3. The relationships in high school are often one of the most important and formative aspects of the teenage years. What do you consider to be the necessary qualities in a friend? Do your friends have these qualities? Do you have these qualities as a friend to others? How can you help your teenager become a better friend to others and develop friendships with those who will help them to be the best version of themselves?

4. What do you know about the spiritual life? Are you able to help your children grow spiritually, or do you need to become better educated in the teachings of the Church? What resources can you find that will help you learn more about the life of prayer and developing an intense personal relationship with Christ?

CHAPTER 7:
THE MODERN ERA: SECULAR ANTHROPOLOGY

1. Doubt and insecurity characterize the modern worldview. They are also common aspects of the teenage experience. How can we help teenagers cope with the challenging emotional aspects of puberty? How can the message of divine mercy help teenagers?

2. The loss of faith is a tragic reality in modern society. What can a school do to help form and educate children in the faith so that they can grow stronger in their relationship with God? How can the school environment and home environment work together to help children grow in the faith?

3. Modern education is focused on the usefulness of learning. What important aspects of the educational experience are lost when the primary focus becomes job stability or wealth creation?

4. G.K. Chesterton and Pope St. John Paul II both offer a remedy to the modern ailment of nihilism. Read chapter 2 of *Orthodoxy* by Chesterton or the introduction to *Fides et Ratio* by Pope St. John Paul II, and discuss what these great apostles of our modern time have to say about the current crisis of faith.

CONCLUSION

1. In the questions for the introduction, you were asked about the purpose of high school. Has your answer to that question changed by reading this book?

2. There is an art to being human, to being alive. We can study and reflect so that we can thrive at the craft of living. Aristotle called this *eudaimonia*. What does a life of flourishing look like

for you? In your opinion, what would be a life of flourishing for your child? How can you help them get there?